"Pulled into orbit. That's how I felt as I opened *Life on Planet Mom*. Like gravity tugging my heart within these pages, I immediately connected with the four fictional characters who introduce each chapter. I also felt drawn to Lisa Bergren, who put into words what I'd always felt as a mom but was not always able to verbalize. On top of that, I greatly enjoyed the input from other moms. This book makes me feel as if I belong to a special club. It also helps me understand why relationships are so needed in day-to-day life on this planet. Good stuff!"

Tricia Goyer, author of *Blue Like Play Dough* and *Generation NeXt Parenting*

"Lisa Bergren gets it! Navigating the joys and challenges of motherhood takes heart, prayer, and a few good laughs, which Lisa provides. She's encouraged me to look beyond my role of mom and stepmom and actually *see myself* again. Wow, what an epiphany!"

Carolyn Castleberry, cohost of CBN's *Living the Life* on ABC Family Channel and author of *It's About Time!*

Also by Lisa T. Bergren

Nonfiction

   What Women Want

   The Busy Mom's Devotional

For children

   God Found Us You

   God Gave Us You

   God Gave Us Two

   God Gave Us Christmas

   God Gave Us Heaven

   God Gave Us Love

   How Big Is God?

Recent fiction

   The Begotten

   The Betrayed

   The Blessed

   Breathe

LIFE ON
PLANET
MOM

a down-to-earth guide
to your changing relationships

LISA T. BERGREN

a division of Baker Publishing Group
Grand Rapids, Michigan

Published by Revell
a division of Baker Publishing Group
P.O. Box 6287, Grand Rapids, MI 49516-6287
www.revellbooks.com

Printed in the United States of America

Library of Congress Cataloging-in-Publication Data
Bergren, Lisa Tawn.
    Life on planet mom : a down-to-earth guide to your changing relationships /
Lisa T. Bergren.
        p.   cm.
    Includes bibliographical references.
    ISBN 978-0-8007-3365-0 (pbk.)
        1. Mothers—Religious life. 2. Interpersonal relations—Religious aspects—
Christianity. I. Title.
    BV4529.18.B473 2009
    248.8′431—dc22   2009002288

Scripture is taken from *The Message* by Eugene H. Peterson, copyright © 1993, 1994, 1995, 2000, 2001, 2002. Used by permission of NavPress Publishing Group. All rights reserved.

The Holmes-Rahe Scale on pages 34–35 is from Holmes & Rahe, "Holmes-Rahe Life Changes Scale," *Journal of Psychosomatic Research* 11 (1967): 213–18, and is used by permission.

Published in association with the literary agencies of Alive Communications, Inc., 7680 Goddard Street, Suite 200, Colorado Springs, CO 80920, www.alivecommunications.com and The Steve Laube Agency, 5025 N. Central Ave. #635, Phoenix, AZ 85012-1502.

For Karen and Hope
with love

Contents

Introduction

It's difficult when we're young mothers—in the throes of momnesia, barely able to remember where we're supposed to be in two minutes (let alone two days)—to plan time for, much less seriously think about, our relationships. We're sleep deprived and pulled in a million directions. We're holding a child or being touched every waking hour. Our daily allotment of words—supposedly so many more than men have—are all used up on phrases like: "Don't touch that!" "Good job!" "Maybe later," "No," "I said no," "Way to go!" "Over here," "All right," "Do you need to go potty?" "But you just went potty," "Say please," and "I'm counting to three!"

Some days it's a struggle just to shower *and* make a meal beyond pouring a bowl of cornflakes we happen to have in the cupboard. I know you agree. Your sisters in the trenches confirmed it when they spoke out in a survey we conducted as part of the research for this book. "I'd love to have more time for my relationships," said my friend Sarah, "but more than that, I'd love to have another hour of sleep right now. My relationship with my child takes every ounce of energy I can find."

So what's a girl to do when she'd love to grab a cup of java with her pals but she's taking her caffeine in shots so she can run the kids around from morning until night? What's a girl to do when she wants to explore her relationship with God, but her prayer life begins—and ends—with "Dear God . . ." and then she's asleep on the pillow? What's a girl to do when she wants to appreciate her mother-in-law and reassure her of the importance of Grammy in her children's lives, but the woman is driving her batty? Hold on, girls, help is coming! I've felt the heart-wrenching pull of competing desires and the weight of expectations and learned to deal with both (fairly well—I think it's a lifelong process of continuing ed!).

As a mom of three, I understand being pulled in a hundred directions. I know what it's like to run, run, run and what it means to be utterly exhausted. We get the eldest off to school, but then the baby is in high-need mode. We get the baby down for his long nap about the time the eldest returns home. Then we're off to soccer, piano lessons, playgroup—on and on it goes. And that hour of sitting and gabbing with the gals—exploring our new relationships as mothers? Uh, it's hard to imagine it, right?

Aah, yes. I too fantasize about weekend retreats with my closest pals; I tune into TV shows that feature friends that are more like siblings—always there for one another, always able to squeeze in a cup of coffee together; I write novels about relationships that are traumatized yet ultimately become stronger. But do I spend the same time and energy on my real relationships? Do all of my relationships survive difficulty? Most of the time.

I want to build better, stronger relationships in all facets of my life, but the tyranny of the urgent (scheduling five dental appointments, doing family budget reviews and bill paying, volunteering for the class field trip, reading a couple books to my preschooler, meal planning, laundry, work, and on and on) usually forces me to delay strengthening my friendships. Family management is a full-time job worthy of a college degree.

Still, the hunger remains. I want real, authentic community. I think. It *sounds* good anyway. But what is it, really, and how do we find and establish it? (We'll seek that out together in this book.) I want relationships that inspire me, hone me, make me a better wife, mother, friend, or just a decent human being. But when I became Mom, I found that every relationship changed. It's as though I went into the hospital as one woman, a citizen of Earth, and emerged as another—on Planet Mom.

Becoming Mom *does* refine and change us forever. It stands to reason that it will refine and change our relationships too. Our responsibilities increase tenfold. We're granted entrance to a special club of mothers and yet feel pulled from the ring of friends who haven't yet ventured into the with-child mode of life. We're validated by parents and grandparents, honored as if we have accomplished a superhuman feat—produced the golden heir!—but now we're watched closely to see if we can do it right.

We may even find we understand our God in a whole new way, feeling a portion of his love that we have never before felt, because it is echoed in how much we love the babe in our own arms.

Of course, before we can tackle and fully explore how becoming a mom has changed all of our relationships—and how to improve on them—we have to find the time and space to see *ourselves* in the mirror again. And after that, our husbands, who for a span of time might become more partner and housemate than lover and true companion.

So, my sister, you who are reading this book, if this sounds a little like your life, take a breath. Becoming Mom has changed you—irrevocably and forever. And it has changed all of your relationships as well. It might be causing some strife for you, if not sheer exhaustion and tears. Or you may feel you have it all together, that you've evolved into your new role, settled into it like a contented hen. (If this is you, may I suggest that you may be a bit like I was, simply not seeing how much better it still could be?)

Here is the good news. I'm not going to lay a bunch of guilt on your shoulders. I'm not going to give you long to-do lists. My goal is simply to help you think it all through, acknowledge what has changed (and what has not), and encourage you to make the most of those changes while discovering your new community on Planet Mom.

In this book, to help illustrate each chapter's topic, I've written a brief fiction introduction, focusing on four friends who are dealing with/celebrating life together. The stories will help us leap into the topic at hand, and, well, being a novelist, I just couldn't resist! Throughout the book we'll stay in touch with Stephanie, Jen, Amy, and Keisha, getting glimpses of their lives (and perhaps a reflection of your own). I hope you'll adopt them as four new fictional friends.

To make the most of this book, I encourage you to take fifteen minutes to read the chapter and another five minutes to reflect on/answer the questions in it. Twenty minutes a chapter—that's all I'm askin'. I know those twenty minutes are precious, but if you want to gain from reading this book, give God the room to grow you and show you what you need to learn; it is really important to take the extra step of responding to the questions. And gold stars for any reader who sits down with other Mamas of the Round Table to talk it through!

Mamas of the Round Table

You can easily use this book as a small group guide and read it one chapter a week. Gather a group of mothers together and meet at alternating homes post-dinner, or at a school, church, or even the local McDonald's or Chick-Fil-A (NOTE: Must Have Indoor Playground), where you can feed your kids and then send them off to play while you talk. At the end of each chapter, you'll find the MOTRT questions for an easy entrée into fascinating discussion. What a great way to make new friends or get to know your friends better!

You'll notice I reference "survey responses" throughout the book; about five hundred women responded to a survey MOPS International and I put out this year. Their stories and insights made me laugh and cry and reminded me about why I love the young-mom community. Such honesty! Such desire to be the best mom possible! Such struggle! Such success! If you were one of our respondents, thank you, thank you for making it through that monster survey. Drawing on the amazing wisdom from those ladies and combining it with my own experiences (and what I've figured out *so far*), I hope that *Life on Planet Mom* provides you with practical assessment and coping tools as well as encouragement for the mothering road.

Becoming Mom is one of the most breathtaking gifts we've all been given, and the little person at your feet or in your arms needs you to pay attention to your life and see it with clarity and hope and vision. She needs you to find joy, even in the midst of the bleary-eyed days. She needs you to get past survival mode and back to really living the life you crave.

I've discovered that in relationship, in heart-bonded, meaningful community, we find a shortcut toward joy, peace, and foundation. Once we feel understood, connected, and known, we find some semblance of satisfaction in this arena.

So come—let's discover together how becoming a citizen of Planet Mom has changed every relationship we have and how life can be as good as (or even better than!) before.

1

Well, Enough About Me. What Do You Think About Me?

how becoming a mom changes you

Being a mom has taught me things about myself I never knew and has given me strength for things I thought I couldn't do (one of my three children is special needs).

Sarah

Being a mom is the most fulfilling job I could ever have. I have two beautiful little mini mes that copy everything I do. It makes me want to be a better person.

Jamie

I feel like I was a diamond in the rough—and I mean rough! My four kids have chipped away at my stony exterior and have revealed a happy, sparkling gem. Each child has helped me see God in a new and beautiful way. It hasn't been easy—that's not how change works—but it has been worth it!

Krystin

W hoa, girl, if you get any bigger, you'll be drinking that soy nonfat chai at the bar instead of in this booth," Stephanie teased, sliding over to make room for Jen.

Jen rolled her eyes and sighed. "Tell me about it." With eleven weeks to go before her second child was born, she couldn't figure out how this baby could find even another inch of room for growth. She smiled over at Amy and Keisha, who smiled back at her in greeting. "This is a miracle, you guys. The Fantastic Four, back together at last."

"It's so great," Amy said. "I've missed you. Between work and families, we never get to see each other, well, you know . . . just us."

Without children, Jen thought. She couldn't blame Amy. In high school they had been inseparable, but now, twelve years later, they had all married and had children—except for Amy. When they did get together, it was hard to stay on any sort of conversation that didn't revolve around the kids. And Amy, although good about it, had to get frustrated. They'd all been glad when Keisha suggested a monthly JGNK Saturday coffee—Just Girls, No Kids.

"Uh, uh, uh," Jen said, shaking her head at Keisha, who was texting someone. "That has to be one of our rules. If we can break away for just one hour, once a month, there can't be any cell phones or texting involved."

Keisha smiled ruefully. "Deal. I just have a client that's on the edge of a cliff. I'm trying to keep him from jumping."

"Talk him down later. It's Saturday. This is our time. An hour—that's all we ask."

"All right, all right." Keisha's eyes moved to Stephanie, who was staring at her coffee, mindlessly stirring it. "Steph? What's up?"

"What? Nothing."

All three of them stared at her. They could see from her startled, guarded reaction that something was most definitely going on with her. Keisha had always been good at that—reading every one of them. That was probably why she did so well at her business.

"Look, we just got here. Can't it wait?"

"I don't know," Keisha said. "Can it?"

Stephanie shoved her brown curls over her shoulder and swallowed hard. Suddenly tears filled her eyes. She started to speak, her lips parting. Then she stopped abruptly, took a sip of coffee, and glanced out the window.

Jen frowned and then scooted closer to her, looping a comforting arm around their friend. "Steph?"

"I-I never could hide anything from you guys, could I?" She smiled through the tears, now cresting her lids. But her friends waited in silence. "He left. Mike left last night. We had an argument and he stood up, turned away, and walked out the door."

"Oh, Steph . . ." Jen said.

"He didn't take anything with him?" Keisha asked.

"Only his wallet." Stephanie blew her nose into the small coffee napkin, and all three of her friends offered her theirs as backup.

"And no word since? No calls?" Keisha asked.

"No," she said, shuddering through her tears. She turned her big brown eyes on all three of them. "I think he's . . . gone. Gone for good."

"No," Amy said, reaching across to cover Stephanie's hands with her own. "There's always hope, sweetheart. He loves you. He loves your boys. You've just hit a rough patch."

"A rough patch of a year?"

"Who has your boys this morning?" Keisha asked.

"Mom."

"Are your mom and Mike getting along any better these days?"

Stephanie's narrow brow wrinkled a bit in irritation. "I don't see what that has to do with anything. My husband left me last night, Keisha."

"I know, babe," Keisha said, softening her tone. "That's gotta hurt, bad. I'm so sorry. But Mike and your mom . . . they go at it, don't they?"

"Sometimes," Stephanie said, shifting in her seat. "They're just so different."

"And last night," Keisha probed gently. "What set Mike off?"

Stephanie paused as if she didn't want to answer. She finally spoke but looked out the window instead of at her friends. "He wanted to come home and not have her there, demanded that she not be there six out of seven nights. It's my home too. She's my mom. I need her. The boys adore her. Why does he have to be so mean?"

The table was silent, all of them wishing to be supportive but wondering how Stephanie could not see the answer. Keisha, as always, was the first to speak. "Do you think . . . would it work for your mom to come over in the mornings instead? The man didn't say he never wanted to see her, right? Only that he wanted you to himself most nights. Is that so terrible—when you have the rest of the day to be with her?"

Stephanie let out a long sigh and rolled her eyes. "If it wasn't Mom, it would be something else."

"Maybe," Jen ventured. "But could you try taking that hurdle off the track?"

Steph's mom had been an issue in their marriage for years. Jen never understood why her friend sided with her mother over her husband time and time again.

"If I offer that, then he's won."

"If you don't, then no one will win," Keisha said. "The big losers? Your boys. Spencer and Ian need their father, Steph. And you need your husband."

Stephanie paused, mulling over Keisha's words. "Maybe you're right. I'll pray about it. You guys . . . I need you to pray for us too, okay?"

"You've got it," Jen said.

"Enough about me and my ongoing marital saga," Stephanie said, lifting a napkin to the corner of her eye and wiping away smeared mascara. "Please, anyone talk . . . about anything other than Mike. How are you doing, Jen? About ready to have that baby?"

Jen sighed. "No way. This baby can stay put until her due date or longer. I have enough on my hands with Nina. I kinda wish we had waited, you know?"

"Too late for that," Amy said.

"Obviously. But I can't help wishing for another year, just with the three of us. Nina's just now getting into some sort of schedule. For the first time, I have a little time for myself. Some space. I played the piano for the first time in a year yesterday. But this little one will arrive," she paused to rub her belly, "and that'll be over."

"Do you know how much I'd love to trade places with you?" Amy said. "A darling little girl, with another one on the way?"

"And an adoring husband?" Stephanie added.

"All right, all right," Keisha said. "You both know Jen better than that." She turned her dark eyes on Jen. "What you need is just something for yourself, right? A place and a time to call your own."

Jen let out a breathy laugh. "I just need to remember who I am. What's important to me, my own dreams and desires. I feel like all I do is manage the household. When I sat down at the piano yesterday, it took a few minutes to begin playing. I couldn't hear it—the music I've always heard."

"I love hearing you play," Keisha said.

"To be able to play like that," Amy said. "By ear . . ."

"But I couldn't hear it yesterday. It scared me. I wondered if it was gone. As if I'd lost it."

"You'll never lose it," Amy said. "It's gotta be like riding a bike for you, playing music by ear."

"But we all get rusty, right?" Keisha said. "I got on a bike for the first time in ten years last week, and for a moment, I wondered if I had forgotten, if I'd fall. I didn't, but I hesitated." She looked back to Jen. "Grab that time for your music," she said. "Every day, when Nina goes to sleep, give her twenty minutes to really be asleep, and then you play, okay? You need it. It'll make you happier, more settled. And you'll see, even with baby number two, you can find those snatches of time for you."

"Promise?"

"I promise. I'll help you if you can't do it on your own."

I love the maternity ward. I mean, not the nurses waking you every five minutes to check your vitals, not the newly excruciating act of going to the bathroom, not the room-mate with no sense of personal space, but the pain meds,

Can you pinpoint a moment in time when you first considered yourself a mom? I mean, a Real Mom? It might have been from the moment you knew you had conceived, or when you walked your child into a preschool classroom—when did you first really identify yourself as a mom?

the room service (whether or not you like hospital food, when's the last time you had breakfast in bed?), nurses willing to take your baby so you can grab a few hours of sleep, visitors to come and adore the baby with you. I love all that. You feel like the star of the show, that you've contributed to society just by producing a living, breathing human being. You want to close your eyes and lean back in exhaustion, still grinning as you feel many hands patting you on the back for your good and glorious work of procreating.

I'll never forget being alone at last in a quiet hospital room with baby number one and waking to discover that she had pooped in her diaper. I reached for the call button, intent on summoning a nurse and a bit irked that my little princess had been allowed to sit in such foul material—black tar meconium. Who knew such terrible things came out of precious, lovely babies? And not only that, she might've been dirty for some time! But as my thumb hovered over the buzzer, I caught myself. I was not the mother of a princess. I was suddenly just the mom. This baby in a poopy diaper was *my child*. And I was *responsible* for changing her diaper, the first of 1.2 million diapers that would follow.

In that moment I think it all came home to me. More so than finding out I was preggers, more so than delivering her and holding her to my breast, it was at that moment when I grasped just how much responsibility I now had, that I was a mom and that I was changed forever. It was almost as if I were a giant clock, and God turned the notched wheel within me ninety degrees. I felt so clearly every click. When he stopped, I was mentally engaged. I assumed my new mantle of momdom.

That emotional engagement was a long time coming; from the time I first saw that blessed stripe on a Clearblue stick, I think I was captivated. (For my friends who have adopted, they've described it as the first time they saw a picture of the baby's ultrasound or locked eyes with the precious one who had somehow always been theirs in a way.) And then to hold that child—finally *hold* her—and get to touch every part of her, nestle her in close. We shot hours and hours of footage of Olivia *sleeping*, for heaven's sake. We were entranced from the beginning and within a week were completely sacked.

Physically I couldn't get enough of her. I was jealous when others held her too much during the day because I ached to get my hands on her. I loved breast-feeding, because it made sure that at least every 2.5 to 3 hours, she was with me and only with me, locking eyes, touching, bonding, connecting. I celebrated when each of my three graduated from newborn blobdom and could smile and coo and reach for me. I liked the weight of a baby perched on a hip or her fuzzy electro hair beneath my chin or twenty pounds of limp flesh sacked out on my chest,

Can you look into a mirror and see YOU anymore? Try it now. How has becoming a mom changed you on the INSIDE? Has it changed you in positive or negative ways?

23

snoring away. I was entranced by the sweet smell of her breath, the fluttering of eyelids as dreams first took shape in her mind, the slight bounce in her soft spot that told me her heartbeat was strong and sure.

Suffice it to say I've loved becoming a mom. I've experienced sheer glory and joy and satisfaction. As so many others have discovered, family is the finest, sweetest gift in my life, after my faith in Christ.

But I can also honestly say there are days I wish I could take off the mom mantle and just be Tim's wife or merely Lisa. I wish I had no other responsibility, that I didn't have to think of anyone else but me, that I could just be me, not someone's mom, 24/7, forever. Those are the hard days, when I feel strung out, pulled in too many directions, the days when everyone needs a piece of me, and I don't feel as if I have any other piece to give, when I concentrate on all that others take from me, rather than all I've been given.

The gifts have been grand indeed. As much as our identity changed when we became the mom, as much as we've given and will continue to give of ourselves in this role, we haven't lost the individual God made us to be. Sometimes we just lose track of her. After a while, though, we look up and catch our reflection in the mirror—and we look beyond the spit-up on our shirts and the grown-out roots that demanded color two weeks ago and into the eyes of a tired but gratified and still-growing woman.

How has becoming a mom changed how you describe yourself? Do you identify with any of the ways listed on p. 25 that mom's lives improve? Circle those.

Becoming a mom has changed each one of us. In our survey 97 percent said becoming a mom had "changed me for the better by 50 to 100 percent." Think of that—an overwhelming majority of mothers believe they have been changed for the better by becoming a mom—and in a significant way.

The ways these mothers reported they'd been changed and "grown" were insightful too. Moms listed such gains as:

responsibility	tenderness
organization	faithfulness
assertiveness	gratefulness
priorities	acceptance
compassion	flexibility
fun	kindness
insight	generosity
nurturing	gratitude
humor	perspective
humility	self-respect

The most common responses were gains in developing the big three: love, patience, selflessness.

Welcome to the Love Fest

I've already described my process of falling in love with my children—which I experienced with each new baby, by the way. Even with colicky baby number two, who shall remain nameless. (Oh, all right, it was Emma, and I'm happy to report she emerged just fine on day one hundred, the day all colicky babies seem to find miraculous healing.) God instills something primal and basic so that we become bonded with these children forever. It's almost as if he opens

25

up our circuitry and hardwires in something new we can't escape because he knows software fails and we'll need a motherboard that will go the distance.

This falling-in-love-with-baby thing isn't always instantaneous. Some of my friends were in love with their child from the second they laid eyes on the little one. Others were so wrung out from horrific labor that they seemed to need a few days to forgive and forget! Author Stefanie Wilder-Taylor writes:

> First off, when that little bun is presented to you fresh out of your oven, you don't even know each other. This is your very first meeting, and it's fraught with incredibly high expectations. That's a lot of pressure. It's like a blind date with a Match.com guy: Up until this point you've only had a rough idea of his height and weight, and a very fuzzy picture to work from. Plus, let's face it, you aren't exactly at your best. You've been in labor, and you are probably under the influence of more drugs than Robert Downey Jr.[1]

But that's just the beginning. As your baby becomes a part of your life, you are destined to know what it means to love in a whole new way. It's miraculous really. We find and choose to love our friends and our mates, but when it comes to children, love simply is part of the deal. Survey respondents described their experience, when it came to love, like this:

"I know a whole new level of love."

"Finally, I understand unconditional love."

"I love more deeply."

"I truly understand what love is."

"My love meter is overflowing."

Doesn't that last one make you smile? All I can picture is a utilities meter going bonkers, the hand rocking around and around as the points add up! Another woman wrote, "I always knew I wanted to eventually get married and have kids. I knew I would love them but had no idea how deep and consuming that love is. It has really broadened my view of life and love and helps me to relate to my heavenly Father even more." Monica said:

> "It has humbled me; it has given me character; it has taught me so much about selfless love. Being a mom has taken me from a place of not knowing what defined me, who I was, or where I was going, to a place of being content with right where God has put me. He has given me my own mission field right here within these walls; it is wonderful to know that he has entrusted me and equipped me with all I need to do the task at hand of training up these three little lives. Before I had kids, all I could think about was myself—where I was, what people thought of me, what I was going to do with my life, and things of that sort."

Many of us have known the love of parents, siblings, friends. Many of us know the love of a man. But holding a child in our arms, staring into his eyes, and knowing that we would give whatever it took to keep him safe, to nurture him, and to see him grow into maturity, is to know love in a whole new way. And in knowing that love at last, we are connected to our parents and our Creator in a whole new way (which we'll explore in later chapters).

You're on My Last Nerve

I love my fellow moms who believe that spending time with their children is the most scintillating, exciting thing they can do. Honestly I wish I could be more like them—they inspire me and tell me that it is possible. But to be perfectly honest, it's taken me some pretty serious work to continually draw from my patience well when it comes to children. For instance, I loved breast-feeding, but after twenty minutes, I was ready for the baby to finish up and move on to burping. I mean, can't we all get a meal taken care of in twenty minutes? I wondered if bottle-fed babies took so long.

As the kiddos got older, other things began to sap my patience—whining, potty training, bickering, the same silly kids' shows, a trail of toys everywhere they went. Frankly, sometimes I still get tired of dealing with kids and wish they'd behave more like adults. Then I look at my friends' children. I can't imagine how they can cope with kids who need no more than six hours of sleep a night or have an inborn monkey trait that makes them want to climb anything possible—banisters, door frames, railings—or won't obey. (I guess God gives us only what we can handle!)

> "Being a mom has stretched me. I didn't know that I could be this patient with people who can drive me completely insane at times or that I could exist on so little sleep. It has taught me the real definition of 'selflessness.'"
>
> *Sheila*

One survey respondent said, "I've learned that I can be extremely impatient one minute and have the patience of a saint the next." Boy, can I relate to that! Eight out of ten times, I find the strength to pull another bucket out of that patience well and carry on. The ninth time I manage to hand children off to my husband before I lose it; the tenth time I blow a gasket. (I figure giving in to fried-dom 10 percent of the time is every mom's right. I mean, we're still human, correct? It's kind of like tithing on a patience scale.) But that 90 percent of the time we have it together—it's amazing what we can deal with.

Do you understand love better now that you're a mom? How so?

I've always said it's way easier to head off to work and negotiate adult problems than it is to spend all day and evening with children, negotiating pint-size issues. Even the biggest crisis at a job is usually resolved in a few days—at most, a few months. Raising children, however, molding them into responsible adults, is a constant, refining process measured in fractions of a centimeter. We gain ground and then we lose it; we reestablish that lost ground and then lose it again. Some days we feel like soldiers crawling up a muddy slope while under heavy fire. And somehow we find the inner strength it takes to get up, put on our helmet, and dive back into the mud the next day.

I liked these other two statements from the survey:

"I've grown more patient, more flexible, more understanding, better able to admit mistakes and apologize for them."

"I'd like to think it's made me more patient, but some days, that's questionable. But it definitely has made me realize I need to stop and think before I speak or act."

It's a humbling thing when I hit that 10 percent blow-a-gasket point and then have to apologize to my children for losing it or overreacting or yelling or exacting punishment that did not fit the crime. But when I do apologize, it resolves hurt feelings faster than anything. It's the great diffuser. After all, if my children wrong me, I demand an apology. How can I do anything else when the situation is reversed? Thankfully, children want nothing more than to love and forgive you. Listen to this story from Betsy:

"Before I became a mom, I was ambitious, driven, self-centered (although I didn't realize it!) and controlling. I had fertility issues, but hey, I had things under control, so medical science could take care of this! After three years of treatments, and finally throwing my hands up to let God have the whole situation, I became pregnant. But God wasn't finished with me. After giving birth to a beautiful boy, I was brought to my knees (no, flat on my back) with postpartum depression. Looking back, I still hadn't learned that God was in control, not me. When you're flat on your back, there is no place to look but up, so I was forced to let God into my world. I had kept him at arm's distance for so long! With the help of a Christian psychiatrist, counselor, friends, and family, I got much better in the months to come. Yet I didn't come out of that valley the same person that I was before. The tight grip that I had on everything that I assumed I could control had to loosen, and my perspective was different. There is a Sara Groves song that says, 'Hope has a way of turning its face to you just when you least expect it.' That hope came in the package of a little boy who is now five years old. While I am supposed to be teaching him, he teaches me so much more about love, forgiveness, and what it means to be human!"

What speaks to me the most in her sweet story is that she had to let go, loosen up, and not try to control everything. These are keys to developing patience in our lives, and mothering gives us ample opportunity to practice them. Just when we think we have a little being we can mold into an image of ourselves, we realize there's only so much we can do. We do our best, over and over again, and then we have to let God do the rest. That's an incredibly freeing bumper-stickerish statement to embrace (at least it has been for me, since I *love* control).

> Do you think you are more or less patient since becoming a mom? Why? How much does "control" drive your mothering style? Is that good or bad?

It Isn't All about Me (Anymore)

The third big thing, after love and patience, that women noted in the survey was how motherhood forces us from being *selfish* to *selfless*. It's a very good thing we find that selfless factor somewhere deep inside. (If you're a new mommy, find it fast, because babies have a way of beating it out of us, like an old woman armed with a carpet beater attacking a dusty Turkish rug she's about to sell.) Don't know what I'm talking about? Think of when you've been on an airplane stuck on the tarmac, trying to quiet a frantic child who needed a nap two hours ago—and shield her from the furious glares of a million fellow passengers. Or how you endured a three-day car trip so she could bond with Grandma. Or how you skipped a fun weekend away because you've been away from your child too much already. Or how you stretch out hair appointments by a couple of weeks so you can finance the perfect children's vitamin. Or how you've gotten up ten times a night to quiet a crying child (or merely to make sure she's still breathing).

You're giving up something *you* want all the time to make your child's life better. I know this because you're a mom.

Collectively, we've given up the perfect job, house, and clothes to make sure our child has the nurturing he needs. Some of us have left states we prefer so that Junior can know his extended family. Others have moved farther away to keep him out of the clutches of toxic relatives.

We think through our hours and days and weeks and months with the child foremost on our mind. Children become the filter through which everything must sift. *If I do this, what will I do with my child? Who will take care of her, if I'm doing that? How will this affect her? Will this benefit her? Will it hurt her?*

"Motherhood has taken me 'off center'—not always putting *my* needs first—really shown me how to find grace in trying situations, and aided me in thinking about the future both long-term and in the present moment."

Julie

As moms, we find ourselves sacrificing for our children over and over, in big and small ways, because it is no longer just about us. "I sacrifice willingly—time, money, resources, self," said one survey respondent. And that movement from selfishness to selflessness is a rounding event, a growth event (an "event" that older mothers tell me lasts a lifetime).

It *Can* Be All about You—at Least Once in a While!

Knowing how to love and give, and doing so in a selfless way, is a sign of maturity. But it is also a sign of maturity to know when you need to take care of you. Becoming a mom doesn't mean you disappear, that you as an individual have disappeared. Becoming a mom is supposed to be a growth thing, an expansion thing. Consider yourself a rough-cut gem. Becoming a mom has just added a few more, huge facets that will get polished and polished and polished until you are shining in whole new ways. But the gem itself? That's still you, Girl.

You've endured some incredibly huge things in these last years. In becoming a mom, you have racked up enough points on the Holmes-Rahe Stress Scale to risk serious illness. It is *critical* that you take care of you! Your children need you!

Holmes-Rahe Stress Scale

As I looked at it, I could see young moms might have a higher chance of hitting those in bold. But you might have encountered even more. Mark each event you've experienced in the last year:

Rank	Event	Value	Score
1.	Death of a spouse	100	___
2.	Divorce	73	___
3.	Marital separation	65	___
4.	Jail term	63	___
5.	Death of a close family member	63	___
6.	Personal injury or illness	63	___
7.	**Marriage**	**50**	___
8.	Fired from work	47	___

Rank	Event	Value	Score
9.	Marital reconciliation	45	___
10.	Retirement	45	___
11.	Change in family member's health	44	___
12.	**Pregnancy**	**40**	___
13.	**Sex difficulties**	**39**	___
14.	**Addition to the family**	**39**	___
15.	**Business readjustment**	**39**	___
16.	**Change in financial status**	**38**	___
17.	Death of a close friend	37	___
18.	Change in number of mar. arguments	35	___
19.	Mortgage or loan over $10,000	31	___
20.	Foreclosure of mortgage or loan	30	___
21.	Change in work responsibilities	29	___
22.	Son/daughter leaving home	29	___
23.	**Trouble with in-laws**	**29**	___
24.	Outstanding personal achievement	28	___
25.	**Spouse begins (or stops) work**	**26**	___
26.	Starting/finishing school	26	___
27.	**Change in living conditions**	**25**	___
28.	**Revision of personal habits**	**24**	___
29.	Trouble with boss	23	___
30.	**Change in work hours, conditions**	**20**	___
31.	**Change in residence**	**20**	___
32.	Change in schools	20	___
33.	**Change in recreational habits**	**19**	___
34.	**Change in church activities**	**19**	___
35.	**Change in social activities**	**18**	___
36.	Mortgage or loan under $10,000	18	___
37.	**Change in sleeping habits**	**16**	___
38.	**Change in number of fam gatherings**	**15**	___
39.	**Change in eating habits**	**15**	___
40.	Vacation	13	___

Rank	Event	Value	Score
41.	Christmas season	12	___
42.	Minor violation of the law	11	___
	TOTAL		___

Score:

<150 points in one year = 37% risk of serious illness in next two years

150–300 points in one year = 51% risk of serious illness in next two years

>300 points in one year = 80% risk of serious illness in next two years

[Responses in bold are author's additions—those I thought you might be even more apt to check off, but read each one!]

Take a moment to mark each event you've experienced on the Holmes-Rahe Stress Scale above. As I went through it, I noted (in bold) events that many young moms are experiencing. But it's worth going down through the whole list, marking each event you've experienced in the last year.

Okay, I didn't add this stress test to wig you out. I don't want to add more stress to your life! But you can see it's important—and not selfish—to take care of yourself. You want to be around for your children for decades to come, right? So the tough question for busy moms is how to work self-care into an already overloaded mix. Here are some of the ways survey respondents noted they take care of themselves:

girls' night out

gym time with childcare

hot showers

bubble baths

crafts

reading

eating right

book club

sleep!

hair appointments

coffee dates with friends

Bible study

shopping alone

Mom's Morning Out

drop-in preschool

MOPS International

surfing the Web

vitamins

kids to bed by 8 p.m.

naptime freedom

women's retreats

daily devotional

pedicures

TV

rising an hour before kids do

walking with friends

Many noted that it helped to have a supportive husband or extended family around to help watch the kids and give them a break, but others noted creative ways to carve out time:

"I put my kids in daycare two days a week—one to work to pay for it, and one for me."

"Rest time is from 1 to 3 daily. I stop *all* housecleaning and read a book or take a nap and don't feel guilty about it, either."

"I read books with 'big' words."

I would often hire young girls to come and play with the kids when I was still at home. You can have an eleven- or twelve-year-old mother's helper for a lot less per hour than if you hire a teen or college student. And having the freedom to take a long bath, surf the Net, read, or even cook dinner uninterrupted can feel like a little break. Keep an eye out for those young girls who obviously love babies and would welcome a chance to gain some experience; tell them you need a mother's helper for a couple of hours a week, and see if they'd be willing to come over and play with your child while you're still home. Establish the rate up front. Voilà—a mini break for you.

Once in a while leave the little darling(s) behind and escape! Run away for a couple of hours or (gasp!) even the whole day. Repeat after me: *Babysitters are my friends. Babysitters are my friends. Babysitters are my friends.* Make it a goal to find a young, wholesome girl you can trust and your children will learn to love. Grit your teeth when the kids wail as you exit, making you feel like you're the worst mommy ever. (They'll stop within five to twenty minutes max and completely forget they were upset, I promise.) Go out alone or with a pal or with your husband. It's good for children to know that when you leave, you will eventually return. They are not abandoned; Mama *will* come home.

> "I take one night away per week, one day away per month, one weekend away per year."

When you go out, enjoy the quiet or adult conversation. Attend a lecture or a concert. Drive country roads without Radio Disney playing in the background.

You've heard it here first: this time is permitted. And it's good for you. You'll return refreshed and ready to be the best mom you can be. (Can't afford a sitter? Trade three hours of sitting twice a month with a girlfriend—you watch her kids, she watches yours.) And self-care is actually an excellent thing to model for your children. (Look, everybody! She's not a mothering robot! She's a growing, changing human being with needs of her own.)

Lisa Whelchel writes in *Taking Care of the Me in Mommy*:

> I can tell you from firsthand knowledge, whenever I did take a bit of time for myself . . . I always came home more in love with my family than when I left. Maybe it is

When is the last time you had three hours to yourself? When is the next time you will? Can you go and make your arrangements now, mark the date on your calendar, so it happens within the next fourteen days? If you are resisting doing this, write down why you feel resistant and pray about it. See if God affirms your view or changes your mind.

the adage, *Absence makes the heart grow fonder.* I don't know. I think it has more to do with the fact that we do love our families so desperately, but occasionally the exhaustion and busyness overwhelms us and we lose sight of this truth. When we pull away from the mayhem, regroup, and refresh, we come back with more to give than if we stayed in the rut, running around in circles, being the "good mom."[2]

And So . . . the Cliff Notes Review

Becoming a mom has fundamentally changed us as individuals, in that it's ripped us all off of selfish moors and placed us on a sea of selflessness (most of the time). In teaching and training the child(ren), we've learned where we ourselves are still lacking, where we still need to grow. But oh, how we've grown already. What a gift this gig is. Motherhood has taught us just what it means to love, really love, and be loved, unconditionally. It's pounded out some measure of patience in our lives. And as we continue to shape the shortest beings in our household, we take a deep breath, look in the mirror, and discover still more about ourselves than we've ever known before. And that's how it should be. Because, in the end, we're still learning and growing too.

Mamas of the Round Table Discussion Questions

1. What has been the most significant physical challenge you've faced as a mom?
2. How have you grown emotionally as a mom?
3. When has mothering been a mental challenge? How so?
4. What part of mothering has personally stretched you the most?
5. What do you hope as a mom to learn to do better in the coming year?
6. How do you plan to take better care of yourself week by week?

2

Who Are You Again?
Oh Yeah, the Guy
I Married

how becoming a mom
changes a marriage

We have to check IDs and wedding bands at the end of some weeks! We have so little time together—that is, when we're both awake.

Monique

On the day we were married, I saw him standing by the altar and thought that I couldn't love him more than I did at that moment. I was wrong. The first time I saw him hold our daughter, I thought my heart would burst wide open.

Chelsey

Things are harder. I want to keep him as number one, but the children's needs seem to come first. By necessity, a poopy diaper has to rank above a sexual encounter.

Stephanie

He expected to continue to do whatever he wanted to do, whenever he wanted. And with children there has to be a plan in place and everything takes more preparation. He resented the loss of spontaneity and became passive aggressive.

Marcie

don't know how you do it," Keisha said, greeting her husband with a hug and a kiss. She glanced over his broad shoulder. Dinner was simmering on the stove and the kids were playing outside, enjoying an uncommonly warm, early spring day. Even little Tyana was toddling after her big brothers, laughing at their antics.

"It's all in how you plan," he said, leaning back and cradling her cheek in his hand. "Girl, you look tired. Sexy as all get-out, but tired."

"I'm whooped," she said, unbuttoning her coat and turning away, hoping Max didn't see it as just the first step in undressing. She was so tired, she didn't think she could get through brushing the kids' teeth, let alone bedtime stories and prayers and the usual bedroom shenanigans. She smiled, imagining herself passed out on the boys' floor, snoring away as they giggled in their bunk bed.

"What's funny?" Max asked, handing her a drink.

"Nothing." She followed him to the couch and sank, gratefully, into it. Max's big, warm hand gently massaged her neck. Keisha closed her eyes, appreciating the warmth and strength of his fingers. She thought of Steph and Mike and wondered if they were doing any better. She needed to give her a call . . . email at least.

"Whoa, getting all tense again," Max said.

"Sorry," she said, giving him a glance from the corner of her eye, not wanting him to stop rubbing her neck. "Here," she said, moving down to the floor, backing up between his knees. "Now you can do my shoulders too."

"You're way too good to me, Mrs. Johnson," he said.

"I do my best, Mr. Johnson. I don't want you to get rusty. After all, if that executive thing doesn't work out for you, at least you can fall back on your masseur skills."

"Only one problem with that."

"Oh?"

"I'd be after only one client." He leaned down and kissed her softly on the neck.

Keisha grinned, moving away as it sent shivers down her back. "Guess I wouldn't want to share my masseur anyway."

The back door opened and the boys ran in, yelling. Tyana came in seconds later, shrieking in imitation. "Mama, Mama, Mama's home!" They ran into her arms, wiry bundles of energy, all knees and elbows in their attempt to love her up. Tyana bounced from one foot to the other, unable to get close to her mother, tears welling.

"All right, all right," Max said, rising from behind her, lifting one shrieking boy onto a shoulder, and then another. "I have no choice but to take you two down. Pile drivers are in order."

"No!" the boys screamed in delight.

"All right, body slams then," their father retorted, carrying them off to the broad expanse of their living room floor to indulge in their nightly WWW reenactment.

"Nooo!"

"What? If I don't body slam you, how will you have room for supper? I need to flatten those little boy bellies . . . now!"

Keisha laughed and welcomed Tyana into her arms. Listening to the boys giggle maniacally as they played with their father, picking dried grass out of Tyana's tight curls as she snuggled close, she was more glad than ever to be home.

She loved her family, loved her husband like crazy. And maybe, just maybe, with a little food energy after dinner, she could stay awake long enough to show him just how much.

For years I carried around the pregnancy test stick that symbolized for me that blessed moment when we knew our lives had changed forever. For me, it symbolized even more than a baby—it was a reminder that life can change in an instant, could have already been changed and I just didn't know it, to expect surprises and shifts on a seismic scale at any time. But as disgusting as it was to carry around an old dried stick that I had once peed on, every time I cleaned out my purse and found it, it made me smile. For my husband and me, becoming parents changed our lives—in three different volleys (Tropical Storm Olivia, Hurricane Emma, and Typhoon Jack). I've named them in storm form (even though all three are very sweet kids) because it was somewhat like that for us; they arrived, and by the time Tim and I looked up, it was as if the winds and the rains had swept through and we were left to reconstruct a new life from the newly shaped pieces.

> "Parenthood has enhanced our strengths. And it has exacerbated our weaknesses. Yet it has given us a new opportunity for deepening intimacy and growth."
>
> *Heather*

A Note to Single Super Moms

You are amazing, admirable, inspirational. You don't know how many times a week I wonder how I would do single parenting, and yet, there you are, doing it. We've included this chapter on marriage, not to leave you out but to address concerns of our married readers. Maybe it will help you dissect what changed in your last relationship, or figure out what you want in your next.

As you once were "eating for two," in the future you may be "dating for two" (or more!). Knowing what you want in a mate—and as a potential father for your child/children—will be a good thing for you to figure out *before* you begin to date. My friend Mamie would never introduce her kids to a man until she had dated him long enough to believe he could really be spouse material (only two men over six years, one of whom became her second husband). I loved that she was both looking for Mr. Right, as well as Mr. Right Stepfather, and protecting her children during the process. Of course, since I've never walked in your shoes, I'll not pretend to be an expert but I can recommend others who are. Check out *Life Interrupted* by Tricia Goyer (teen pregnancy) and *My Single Mom Life* by Angela Thomas.

And if you're in that awful place of hurt and abandonment or struggling to heal or just trying to make it through each day without cracking—*it's so much to handle alone!*—know you are *not* alone. Groups like MOPS (Mothers of Preschoolers), your local churches, even the community paper often advertise single parent support groups—be sure to connect with one if you don't already have the support you need. There are options for you.

This prayer may give you comfort:

Creator God, you are the Maker of each of us. You knew me in the womb, just as you knew my child. This was not the life I imagined, but it is my life, our life. I thank you and praise you for the gift of my child, for the privilege of being a parent. Help me make the most of our life together. Help me find time and energy to enjoy my child, to laugh with him. Help me to find others who are willing to be a part of his life, so that he can see healthy family relationships modeled firsthand. Help me to know how to connect my child with his father and to other good father figures. Help me, Lord. Sustain me. Ease my loneliness. Wash away my pain. Forgive me my failures. Hold me. Love me. Fill me. Teach me. Guide me. Protect me. I accept what lies behind me and where I am today and look forward to what is to come. With you, I am never, ever alone as a "single" parent. Amen.

We Bergrens are not alone in experiencing the drastic changes that children bring. In the survey others indicated they felt the same way:

82 percent said that having a child had made a 50 percent change or greater in their marriage (good or bad)

46 percent felt there had been an 80 percent change to their marriage (good or bad)

59 percent felt much closer to their husband

26 percent felt somewhat closer to their husband

63 percent felt parenthood had distanced them from their husband ("often" and "sometimes" combined)

Sometimes, as young parents, we're too storm-ravaged to really register what has happened, and it takes years to discern what has shifted, in good or bad ways. But it is important to pay attention to the changes, to celebrate positive effects, and to be on top of negative shifts so they can be gently put back on course.

Parenting Can Draw You Closer Together

Parenting is a grand adventure and can often bring two parents together in a whole new way. For biological parents, there is no finer thing than to gaze on a child and recognize that this magnificent creature is the product of their love. For adoptive parents, there is something sacred about bringing a child home as well, grafting that child into their lives, so that she becomes part of the family as clearly as if she had been born into it.

I love what Heather says about "deepening intimacy and growth." Herein lies our greatest opportunity with our spouse. But utilizing one of the most stressful and monumental changes in your lives to lead to that deepened intimacy and growth takes work, intentional work, and from both parties. I know, I know. You're *tired*. I get that. But don't let it overwhelm you. Think of it as redirecting a stream as opposed to stopping a river. If you build little sandbag walls here and there, it will send your marriage in a whole new direction. But if you don't sandbag now, that river can run wild.

The most important aspect of this is having time with your husband to talk, not only to talk about the game plan for the day and how you're going to manage it—or to spill your frustration after a long day of struggling to work that plan and failing—but also to talk in a bigger-picture manner. It's essential to have time and space to discuss issues that are bothering you, ways your children need to be guided/taught, future plans, your marriage, how each of you is faring, how you are growing (or stagnating), what each one needs, and how you might help each other meet those needs.

What about you? Would you say parenthood has made you feel closer to your husband or more distant? Why do you think this is?

Tim and I often get into a "divide and conquer" mode. With three kids and each of us with our own careers, we seldom have a choice. I feel like a coach with the clock ticking down: "You've got him; I've got the girls; go, go, go!"

While I love that we're in partnership on this parenting track, our parenting tasks don't develop intimacy and growth. No, they just accomplish our day-to-day family management. Tim and I are both dreamers, long-range, big-picture people, so we need time to sit and think in big ways—where we might live in the future, the kind of house we might build, grand foreign places we want to see before we die, things we'd like to do if we have the time and energy. You get the idea. We don't have the time and energy to tackle those things now, but just talking about them invigorates us, excites us, brings us together. What would do the same for you and your hubby?

> "There is nothing left of me at the end of the day. I have to force myself to pay attention to his needs. Not just sex, but he used to get back rubs and foot rubs and now? Hello. I am the one who needs that. Do I get one? No."
>
> *Jolene*

To be fair, I should tell you that Tim and I also spend a fair amount of time talking over parenting and the kids. We talk about what is working, what is not. We cover subjects from self-esteem to lying to chores. And we try to be open to the other's constructive criticisms and observations. But when we get stressed, often it's not pretty around the Bergren household. Despite our best efforts to refrain, we lash out at the kids or each other, venting. And then the kids do the same! (You wouldn't want to be

What's a sandbag wall you could be building right now that would move your family's river in the right direction? What's a sandbag wall you could build that would send your marriage on a slightly better course?

coming for dinner on those days, trust me.) Because we both do work that has deadlines, we spend a fair amount of time talking about how we might take on more parental/household responsibilities when the other is under the gun. And that's a good example of the sandbags I'm talking about—recognizing a stress point and figuring out a plan *ahead* of time to redirect the river, rather than letting it wash over you (and potentially carrying one of you away).

While laying sandbags might be more of a shoulder-to-shoulder partnership act, not particularly intimate, it does allow you to be in deeper discussion with your husband about your family's and marriage's direction. Planning in partnership, trying to focus the flow together, can be deeply gratifying and encouraging, helping you grow together through the act of parenting.

There's nothing more overwhelming than trying to parent in ways that oppose how your spouse is trying to parent. In seconds the river is overflowing its banks and seeping into your basement. My parents always, always stood together as a united front, even if they had to "discuss" things later in private in greater detail. As a child, I hated that. I called them the Unit and was frustrated I could never work them, get what I wanted by going to the other parent when the first said no. But I also found comfort in the Unit—kids always crave boundaries, despite what they say, and they love it when parents are together, unified, co-operating. It makes them feel safe, cared for, watched over, loved. Together, you can create great boundaries that will keep your children safe and on a path of healthy growth. And in turn, your marriage will grow too.

You can also find greater intimacy with your husband through your shared love for your child. Learn to adopt some of the love he's showing your child as love for you too. After all, you know how much parenting takes out of you. Children can be huge love-and-care-seeking-suckers that leave us dry and shriveled on the kitchen floor, can't they? When my husband takes the kids out back and plays with them, or he talks through some tear-inducing subject with our teen, their bonding resonates with me. It's like cartoon radio waves reaching out in big arcs and flooding over me. I can't help but smile—and appreciate that I can experience his love from afar.

> "The first time I heard him talking to our newborn daughter over the baby monitor, I just about died with love for him all over again."
>
> *Sasha*

Others from our survey described how parenting has grown their marriages:

"It's a new opportunity to truly understand each other."

"It's added another layer to our relationship."

"We depend on each other more."

"It's expanded our prayer life."

"We've matured."

"It's taught us to work together."

"It's given us a new bond."

"We appreciate each other more."

Twelve Ways Parenthood Can Draw You Closer

1. Commit to getting the kids to bed by 8 p.m. each night so you and your husband have some time awake together.
2. Read a parenting book together, aloud, when the kids are in bed. Discuss what you read.
3. Find parenting techniques you both agree on; it is oddly gratifying to hear your husband backing you up by parenting in the same way you do.
4. Pray for each child with your husband, and ask God to help you be the best parent possible.
5. Date night: go out at least twice a month; commit to discussing the children for no longer than half of your time together. (Other discussion starters can be found on page 61.)
6. Celebrate together your child's growth—whether he learned to tie his shoes or he told the truth.
7. Discuss what you think each child needs to learn, and what you both need to be teaching your child in your own unique ways.
8. Consider how your child is echoing your own behavior and mannerisms; be open to how this might be a negative reflection that you should change—for you, for your spouse, and for your child.
9. Family dinners: they really are important. It may be macaroni and cheese at the kitchen table, but sit down every night that it's possible, as a family, and chat about your day while you eat.
10. Send funny emails to your husband at work (or get him to send you funny emails at your work) about great things the kids say.
11. Have sex once in a while, even if you don't feel like it—your husband will appreciate that you're prioritizing his needs above the family's. (More on this subject later in the chapter.)
12. Dream about your child's future together. What are you working for? Do you want to pay for her college education? Do you want her to travel around the world? Spend time with extended family? Together, invest in today to make the most of her tomorrow.

"This joy has brought us together."

"We share this constant sense of amazement."

These quotes make me smile. Hurrah!

Parenting Can Drive You Apart

Of course, as much as parenting has the potential to draw you and your husband closer together, there's also a downside. Here's what some survey respondents said about how parenting has negatively affected their marriages:

"I can see him as just another obligation."

"All we talk about is our child."

"Difference in parenting styles has separated us almost to the point of divorce."

"I'm exhausted and unable to focus on my marriage."

"We're stressed."

"I've felt isolated from birth to the end of breast-feeding."

"He's no help at all, doesn't want to get involved."

"I'm not the fun-loving girl he married; I'm tired."

"Reconnecting is hard."

These words make me feel weary and I'm not even in the throes of babydom any longer. The three most common things that survey respondents said had driven them away from their mate were *time, energy,* and *prioritization.* And all three are interconnected.

Time

Time is definitely a challenge, particularly if you have more than one child, your mate is a workaholic (or on deadline), or you both work. If time is your particular area of contention, you have to schedule in time for each other. I mean it. You have to put the date on the calendar, on both of your calendars. Block out time and space each day and do something special each week and something really special each month. These guidelines can be flexible when one of you has a big project or deadline, but talk about it together and determine what you will allot to marriage care. During particularly stressful months or years, this might mean you are spending fifteen minutes in daily, uninterrupted conversation, which is at least something.

Figure out habits that help bond you together, without taking a lot of time. Tim and I have found it's good for us to spend a minute hugging in the morning, once we're both up and vertical. It's a great, reassuring way to start my day that connects me to him, and it takes all of sixty seconds to start our day out right. I talked to one mom who had great success, after time, getting her kids to wait to talk to their dad until she and her husband had had twenty minutes of uninterrupted conversation on the couch together. (When I tried this, my children just stood on the sidelines looking like vultures held back from fresh carrion—highly distracting—but hey, you can try it! It worked for her!) Another woman I met has

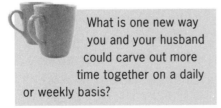

What is one new way you and your husband could carve out more time together on a daily or weekly basis?

her husband call her on his cell while he battles traffic to get home—they redeem that otherwise frustrating time to talk about both of their days before the children and evening chaos descend.

Energy

Oh, but you say you can find ways to eke out some time for your man, but you have no energy. Sister, I totally understand. I love sleep. Bed is an entity to me. I say "bed" with a breathy, dreamy tone. One of the happiest parts of my day is slipping between the sheets. My grandmother told my husband, shaking her finger in his face, "You remember, she needs her sleep!" And during the baby years, it took a very long time to get under those sheets—or I was pulled out from under them far too often (one word: *colic*)—and I began living in a semi-dream state, going through the motions of the day but constantly exhausted.

> "At the end of the day I am exhausted from the daily routine. When my husband gets home from work I have no energy or brain power left for him."
>
> *Kathy*

There is no easy way to say this. The exhausted months/ years are something you just have to endure, make it through the best you can. When a baby is crying or sick, and so is his sibling, sleep is going to become a premium in short supply. But also hear this: it comes to an end. One day you will again get a full night's sleep. And in the meantime, you can do things like take naps along with your children and bail on using the dishes—going with paper once in a while. (Yes, you can still be a good mother and serve dinner on plastic!) You can organize so you're shopping and

What three decisions or requests could you make right now that would leave you an hour of energy for your husband every night?

running errands fewer times a week—whatever it takes to conserve every morsel of energy. Bring your husband into this process. Give him errands to run. Tell him things have to be different for a while, because you're absolutely wiped. Here's a sample script:

"Sweetheart/Lovebug/Hero, I need your help. This mothering deal is almost killing me. I'm so tired. So for a few months [or until some milestone is reached—like your child sleeping through the night], I need you to be ready for some changes around here. I can't keep the house like either of us would like it. I need you to bring home dinner a couple nights a week. And if you can do _____ and _____ each week—make that your personal responsibility—it would really help. Can you work with me on this? I would appreciate it so much."

If he says no on your specific suggestions, ask him, "Okay, I understand that. Can you think of two other things you could pick up and carry for a while instead?"

Men love to help *fix* things. Give your man the opportunity. Also, if you can afford it, see if you can hire a maid service for a period of time. Ask if your mom or another relative can come and sit with your child while you take a long bath/long walk/long nap. Check out your local Dream Dinners or Super Suppers—the stores where you sign up, go and make twelve meals, and bring them home to your freezer. You can't believe how much time and energy that will save you!

What else could you do that would help you conserve energy for your husband and child(ren)? Think on that for a minute and then go and make some calls. I mean now. Yes, now. Three minutes now will gain you an hour of increased energy down the road, I promise.

Prioritization

Perhaps prioritizing is your particular issue. If so, you're not alone. Listen to what your fellow moms had to say:

"I have to share him now, and that can be hard at times. I am not the first one he greets when he walks in the door after work, and sometimes we can go an entire evening (or *week* of evenings) without getting in a real, actual, meaningful conversation. We have to make a lot more of an effort to be close to each other, physically and emotionally, than we did before having kids."

Carody

"I constantly fight the battle to put him number one now."

Leslie

"We have to make time for each other. When we started feeling like roommates instead of husband and wife, we sought counseling. It helped some, but I think we just have to make time alone together and share fun experiences, things that are only ours."

Jill

"He comes in second most times, third more times than not (two kids)."

Jeanne

"He has taken a backseat unfortunately. He has a lot less of my attention, my energy, and a lot less sex."

Teresa

It's so hard for young mothers to understand how important their marriage is to their children. If you are unhappy or dissatisfied (or your husband is), it's going to filter through to your other relationships. It's very important to focus on your marriage and do what you can to get it on track. (God—self—spouse—family—friends—world is really a great priority list, which we'll explore more in detail later in the book.)

But this chapter is about your marriage, and I want to encourage you by telling you that parenthood is not the end of your intimate relationship with your husband; it's just another stepping stone. So how do you reconnect with the man who could become more a roommate than lover? Sharon says, *We are more busy with our kids and their activities. We don't have time alone like we used to. There are days (many of them) when all of our conversations are about activities and logistics. We don't have as much time to just talk and be together. I miss my husband!"*

I know that feeling. But all is not lost. Here's how I've rediscovered my mate along with the advice of others to boot.

How to Rediscover Your Mate

Appreciation is huge. If you are feeling unappreciated for your efforts, you're going to start feeling bitter, which will evolve into anger and all sorts of unpleasantness. If your man doesn't appreciate you (or you think he doesn't), you need to talk it through. Don't go the accusation route—"You don't appreciate all I do around here!"— think sandbag/river route control. Here's what I'd say: "Honey, I'm sure you don't mean to do this, but [*this specific action*] makes me feel unappreciated. I work so hard, even though you might not see all I do, and I need you to understand that I need [*this specific thing*]."

Not only do men love to fix things, they also like to have *specific goals*. Don't go all vague and girly on your husband. Tell him exactly what you need, when, and how. Not particularly romantic, I know, but we're talking manspeak. You have to learn it and appreciate it for what it is (and isn't) to improve your communication and your relationship. And he will need reminding on occasion, but never haranguing. Tell your best girlfriend what you're going to ask your man to do, and tell her not to let you ask him about it again for a minimum of three months. (*Note*: Sometimes changes in behavior are slow. Be patient and prepared to wait. And pray

"There was a time I was feeling unappreciated and unwanted. I was beginning to think we should not be married because I didn't think he was helping and didn't think he cared about me. That was totally wrong, but we hadn't spent any time alone together without kids in over a year, not even for dinner. We were lucky because our church started offering date night once per month on Friday nights. You could drop your kids off at 6:15 and then pick them up at 8:30 for free. That two hours planned time gave us the break we needed to talk about what was going on with us individually and as a family. That date night routine saved my sanity and our marriage."

Dana

59

about it too. Rather than nagging your hubby, nag God. He can take it. And he wants to hear about our needs and desires.)

Men are also inspired by modeling. No, I'm not saying you have to look like the models in *Vogue*. I'm saying that if you crave appreciation and wish your husband would occasionally say, "Thanks so much for taking such good care of our kids," or "I can't get enough of macaroni and cheese for dinner," then tell him what you appreciate about what *he* does each day for you and your family. It might be bringing home the bacon or cutting the grass or making dinner or running the kids somewhere—but *tell him* what you're thankful for.

Here are other ways women from our survey have reconnected with their DH (dear husband):

honest conversation

date nights

respect

turning off the TV

speaking his love
    language (see p. 61)

being more playful

laughing together

porch time on the swing

reading together

coffee in the a.m.; ice
    cream in the p.m.

cuddling

making love

enrolling in a marriage
    class

bike rides

watching/discussing
    movies

setting aside busy work
    to concentrate on him

taking a jacuzzi

reading Song of
    Solomon (in the
    Bible) together

recalling how we
    fell in love

reading a daily
    devotional together

**Ten Discussion Starters
That *Do Not* Center
on Children**

1. What is the scariest thing you've ever done? Would you do it again?
2. What challenge would you like to meet in the next year? Can we challenge each other to meet our personal goals?
3. What is your proudest accomplishment? What are you proud of right now?
4. If you could choose another career, what would you do?
5. When was the moment you first knew you loved me?
6. If money were no object, what are the top three places you'd like to see in the world? Can we start saving a little money to see one of those in the coming years?
7. If you were a billionaire, what charities would you give money to? Can we give a small amount to each of those over the course of this year?
8. What do you think defines an excellent marriage? How can we get closer to that ideal?
9. Describe your ideal day to me. Can we make that happen for you in the next three months? Can we schedule it in? Can we do the same for me?
10. Do you know what I appreciate most about you?

Other ideas are listening to marriage experts together on iTunes, reading Gary Chapman's *The Five Love Languages* and discussing it—Chapman outlines how we perceive and give love in five main ways and how you might not be speaking your spouse's love language (or he might not be speaking yours!), or getting a pack of discussion starter cards to work through together.

And yes, you really should have sex once in a while.

The Doctor Said We Shouldn't Have Sex for Six Years

Okay, so most doctors ask us to refrain from sex for "six weeks" rather than "six years" to allow moms to heal postlabor. But rediscovering your libido when you've been touched by a small person all day is not always easy . . . and can take some time. There have been months when I believed that I really didn't care if I ever had sex again; I'd been touched and loved on enough, not to mention that when I went to *bed* (remember the dreamy, breathy way I say the word?), I was thinking *sleep* not *sex*.

And yet . . . and yet . . . there has never been a time when my husband seduced me out of my weariness and into his arms that I've regretted it. Afterward I am inevitably gratified and reconnected to my husband. As Susan said, "Sex—a mom friend further down the path gave me some great advice: 'It only takes ten minutes, and it makes him so happy.'" And done right, it will make you happy too! (*Helpful hint*: Buy some fantastic smelling massage oil and playfully "trade" him a ten-minute massage for sex. It changes it from feeling like just one more obligation to a gift from your husband.)

Sometimes it's just a matter of letting yourself get in the right frame of mind. I've always carried a torch for male stars who are dedicated family men—husbands and fathers who are committed to their clan. Their dedication was sexy to me. And when my own husband is sweet and kind and playful with my kids, it stirs me too. I'm not alone in this—numerous people on our survey noted fatherhood as "sexy." So tap into that source of inspiration, if it turns your crank!

But exhaustion and what I affectionately refer to as "over-touching" by small ones are not the only things that get in the way of doing the happy dance. We women can let hurt feelings or a sensation of distance between us

> Are you having sex as often as you would like? Are you having sex as often as your husband would like? Why or why not? Is there something you can do to remove any obstacles?

and our husband separate us even more when we refuse this most intimate of acts. Anger and frustration, allowed to linger, become sandbag walls that direct your sex-life river into a vast, cracked-soil desert where it all but disappears. Take the time to diagnose what's really behind your lack of interest in sex, if that's your issue, and then address those things.

The Eleven Year Itch

The key to a successful marriage is to accept that it is an evolving, living relationship, bound to change, not just now but again next year and in ten years. Elisa Morgan and Carol Kuykendall say in their book *Children Change a Marriage*:

> The fact is, just as marriages naturally grow and change as we go through transitions in life, so does the way we experience and express our love for each other. The romantic passion of new love eventually grows into the stage of comfortable love, which grows into the stage of deeply committed love. And in between are inevitable times of numb love or dull love or quiet love.[3]

63

I love that last line about *numb*, *dull*, or *quiet* love. If you're anything like me, those times cause alarm bells to ring and I hear a tiny woman in my head shrieking, "Get thee to a marriage counselor!" instead of trusting in the covenant and foundation of our great marriage. There are seasons in a marriage that come and go; you just have to adjust to the new climate for a time.

I hit the seven year itch about year eleven (I'm slow, sometimes). It was that year that I looked up and stared at my husband and thought, *So. Hmmm. Is this all there is? Well. It just isn't what it once was, is it?* I wrestled and prayed through several months of dissatisfaction and concern that our marriage seemed, well, rather boring, rote, humdrum. There was no big issue, no problems. Tim was not abusive and he was doing nothing wrong. I was just *bored*. So I committed to praying that God would reignite my appreciation and passion for Tim, that I would see new things in him and in our marriage that would bring me satisfaction and enjoyment.

The good news is that God is faithful. It's never ever a bad thing to change worries and concerns into prayers asking for help. The more I prayed those prayers, the more I saw Tim in a new light, discovered things about him that I appreciated, enjoyed hanging out with him, loving him. We reinstituted date night and began dreaming about our future again. We ventured out and found ways to laugh and learn new things together. And slowly the boredom faded.

Prayer is always a good idea in a marriage. When I asked author and speaker Gary Thomas what the most important aspect of faith was, when it came to marriage, he said, "Prayer. Start praying and keep praying for each other.

When I pray for my wife, specifically asking God to help her face her struggles as a mom, it gives me empathy and understanding, while also delightfully assaulting my expectations. It makes me pull for her, instead of fall prey to the temptation to resent her. Pray for each other; even better, pray with each other."

In the same way, we can pray for our husband, asking God to help him in his struggles as a father. Here's a start on that prayer: *"God, I need your help. You know my mind and heart are consumed with my own concerns as a mother. I ask you to reach out to my husband and help him be the best father he can be. I ask specifically that you encourage him in this way: _____"*

No doubt about it, kids change your marriage forever, but hopefully, it can be in a good way. Think about what has changed and what has not. Identify the things on which you need to concentrate and work through. Your union with your husband is important, so seek counseling or wisdom from older married friends, if you feel lost. You might feel like your relationship is on "the back burner," as one woman put it, but you can make the choice to move it forward again.

Mamas of the Round Table Discussion Questions

1. How has becoming parents improved your marriage or made you feel closer to your husband?
2. Are you and your husband able to stand together as a couple when it comes to disciplining your children, establishing rules, or teaching them? Why or why not? How could you draw even more together on these fronts?

Wisdom on Relationships

Gary Thomas is a great resource and has many wise things to say on all familial relationships. Here's a bit more of our brief, email conversation:

LTB: Gary, what advice do you give to young couples struggling to adjust—not only to parenting but also to the changes parenthood has brought to their marriage?

Gary: Now that two of our children are in college, and only one is still at home, I am so grateful that Lisa and I kept growing our marriage, or this would be a truly frightening time. It is natural to become infatuated with children; part of it is a God-given process to bond us to our offspring, who will soon test our patience. But just as feelings shouldn't govern romance, they also shouldn't govern our priorities in building a family, and that means keeping the marriage intact and growing even when you are really "into" your kids and hate the thought of leaving them even for a single night.

LTB: How do we do that, specifically?

Gary: One rule we live by is to be kind to each other. When a wife is tired, feeling in need of a shower after a long day of watching the kids, and the husband grows impatient because one little thing was overlooked, it can really begin to tear apart a marriage. Or a wife knows she is neglecting her husband, but she figures he'll understand and continues in her neglect, in any number of areas. I would tell every young parent: every day, wake up and ask God, "How can I be kind to my spouse today?" What better model to give to your kids than this?

Gary L. Thomas is the bestselling, award-winning author of *Sacred Influence: How God Uses Wives to Shape the Souls of Their Husbands; Sacred Marriage, Sacred Parenting*; and most recently, *The Beautiful Fight*. (If you don't have time and energy to read a whole book right now, do yourself a favor and check out his devotionals, *Devotions for Sacred Parenting* or *Devotions for a Sacred Marriage.* You could even read them once a week with your hubby!)

3. If you are a single mom or are currently separated from your husband, and if you feel comfortable doing so, please share how you deal with daily life without the support of a spouse.

4. Do you have quality time with your husband? How do you carve out this time? What are some ways you can do that more consistently?

5. Have you experienced the "Is this all there is?" question in your marriage? If so, how did you weather it? If not, how would you weather it, should it occur in the future?

6. What are the biggest obstacles to your feeling closer to your husband today? Any ideas on how you could remove those obstacles or at least chip away at them?

7. For single moms in the group: whom do you seek out the most as your chief supporter, encourager, and listener? For married moms in the group: would you go to the same person in your life, if you were single? If not, whom would you choose?

3

My Family Tree Is Suddenly a Forest

how becoming a mom changes your relationship with your family of origin

We had difficulty conceiving a child and my sibling could not understand the heartache of that situation and still does not understand the needs of someone who stays home with children.

Kim

There have been challenges that have required adjustments in the relationship. We have struggled to evolve from a parent-child relationship into an adult-adult relationship with both sets of parents.

Betsy

My sisters don't understand why I can't just drop everything and go out for drinks with them.

Angie

I feel closer to my parents than before. I have a greater appreciation for the way they raised my sister and me, nurtured their marriage relationship, and allowed God to lead their lives.

Michelle

S tephanie bit the cuticle from her thumb as she paced before the front window.

"He's not due for hours yet," her mother said, dropping a load of laundry on the couch to fold.

"I know," she said, turning and joining her mother. "I don't think the clock has ever moved this slowly." She folded a towel and then dared a look toward Ellen.

"Mom, I think it would be best if you were gone when he arrives. Why don't you let me finish this and you head on home?"

Ellen's lips clamped tightly shut and she flung out a towel to straighten it with more force than necessary. "The man's been gone three days, not three weeks."

"That's three days too long."

"He shouldn't have left in the first place."

"I know that. He knows that. We'll work through it. But neither of us needs you to remind us of the facts, Mom."

Ellen placed the towel, neatly folded, on the arm of the couch. "Heavens, I don't want to be in the way," she said, rising. "The last place I want to be is somewhere I'm not wanted."

"Mom," Stephanie said tiredly, "we've been through this. I love you. Please. Sit down for a minute."

Ellen paused, as if teetering on the edge of decision, then at last sat down. This was typically the hour they sat and had coffee together, with Spencer still in school, and Ian clinging to his afternoon nap. Sometimes they'd play cards, sometimes they'd start dinner, sometimes they'd garden, sometimes they'd watch a talk show. It just depended on the day.

"Mom," Stephanie said, taking her mother's hand, as the marriage counselor had encouraged. "I know these last years have been tough on you. Losing Dad has been terrible. And you have been a huge help to me, with the kids, keeping me company, helping me run this house. I don't want to lose you. I don't want to lose us. You're too important to me. And Mike . . . while he hasn't always been nice to you, I know he loves you too."

Ellen let out a snort and tried to pull her hand away.

"No, Mom. Wait. I think what's happening is that Mike just wants to know what it means to be our immediate family. And I think . . . I think . . ."

"What? Just say it."

Stephanie sighed and plunged forward. "I think it might be good for you to explore what it means to be just you. Alone, in your house some. Or out in the community."

"I spend plenty of time alone." Ellen succeeded, this time, in pulling her hand from her daughter's. But she didn't move.

"It's been five years, Mom, since Dad died. I'll say it again—I want you to be a big part of our lives, my kids' lives. We all love you. But we need some time apart too. For all of us, I think it would be best."

Ellen rose and wrung her hands together. "How much time? A week? A month?"

"No, no, no," Stephanie said, rising too. She ran her hand through her long, curly hair, playing with the ends. *Why did this have to be so hard?* "I was just thinking that, for instance, tomorrow you'd go out on your own instead of coming here. Call a friend up and meet her for lunch. It's been forever since you've seen Carol, right?"

"Carol and I have nothing in common."

"You were best friends, Mom. She's been a widow for three years—three years she could've used your company, since you know what it's like."

"You needed me too, after Ian was born. My responsibility was to you, first."

"I did need you. You've saved me, Mom, in more ways than one. But now, now I need to stand on my own. And you do too."

"So this is it? We're saying good-bye?"

Stephanie sighed heavily. "No, Mom, I'm just saying let's see each other half as often, which is twice as often as most mothers and daughters I know. I think this is too much, too close. I think Mike feels shut out, with all our inside jokes and shared experiences that we talk about at dinner. I need to find more ways to share those with him."

"So this is my fault. Your separation."

"No, it's mine," Stephanie said wearily. "I wasn't aware. I couldn't find the energy to care. And I didn't want to give you up. You make my life easier in so many ways. But it's best for all of us if we just take two steps apart from one another. I'm almost thirty years old and I've never lived more than three miles away from my mother. "

"Lots of women are like that."

"Not a lot. Not anymore."

Ellen started to say something, then closed her mouth. At last she said, "So . . . what are you imagining a week would look like, in this new scenario?"

Stephanie smiled a little, recognizing that her mother was at least opening her mind to the idea. "I was thinking you'd come over every

Sunday for dinner, that I'd bring Ian over to your house once a week, instead of your being here all the time. I could teach you how to use that computer that's never been out of the box. Spencer would miss his Grammy if he didn't get to see you, so maybe you could come over here twice a week, after lunch for a few hours, so he could get home, show you his homework, and share a cookie with you. But then it would be just us."

"Without me."

Stephanie swallowed hard, past the lump in her throat that formed at the sound of her mother's sorrow. "We'd be with you four out of seven days a week."

"But not all day on those days."

"Right. Not all day. For some of the day. That's still a lot, Mom. Could we try it for a few weeks? See how it feels? I'm not saying that we do it forever. I'm saying we try it on for size."

Ellen walked stiffly to the front door and pulled her coat from the hook. She looked ten years older all of a sudden, and Stephanie had to bite her tongue and physically hold herself back from going to her, begging her to stay. But she knew she had to try this, as the counselor had insisted.

Her mother reached down for her purse and pulled the strap over her shoulder, waiting, as if she expected Stephanie to stop her. When she didn't, she turned to the door and pulled it open, staring into a cold spring wind, the breeze lifting her gray hair slightly from her forehead.

"So then," she said, pulling leather gloves from her pocket and sliding them on, "I'll come over on Sunday for dinner. You'll call me, tell me what I can bring?"

"I'll call you tomorrow."

Ellen glanced in her direction. "I love you, Steph. I know it took a lot for you to say something. We'll work this out. And you and

Mike . . . you'll work it out too. You know I'm praying for that, right? Praying for you two? Your marriage? I never wanted to be, you know, in the way."

"I know, Mom."

Ellen lifted her gloved hand to her lips, kissed her fingertips and blew in Steph's direction, just as she had since she was a little girl. And then she was gone. Stephanie moved to the window and watched as her mother pulled out of the driveway and drove slowly down the street.

Steph glanced at the clock—only two hours to go until Mike got home.

Hopefully for the night.

Hopefully for forever.

Roots Go Deep: Parents

I'll never forget holding my sweet little seven-pound newborn in the football hold, not only to breast-feed her but so that *I could also mop the kitchen floor with one hand.* Uh-huh, you read that right. I'm shaking my head at myself, thinking what a sorry excuse for a woman I was in that desperate hour. But you see, my MIL (mother-in-law) was about to visit. And where I come from, a clean and tidy house is part of what defines a good woman. (It's taken years to beat that partially out of my addled brain.) My MIL did not expect it of me; I expected it of myself. When my maternal grandmother visited and delighted in the fact that my house was "so clean," I was disgustingly happy with myself. Thirteen years later it still gives me a chill of pleasure and delight that I met the matriarch's approval. Sick, I know . . .

But we enter into parenthood with a series of tapes running through our head, good and bad, and they often deal with subjects that are bigger than how one cleans one's house. It's important to take them to the editing room and consider what footage you want to keep around, now that you're a mom and laying down rough cuts for your own children. For instance, it was a lot easier keeping a nice, clean house when there was only one baby, and she did not yet crawl. Three kids, a dog, and an artist husband, who drags in fragments from the garage, have beaten my neat freak tendencies down to a dull, frustrated roar. And that's okay; I've realized that how I keep my house no longer defines me. Nor do I want to spend hours a day on the unending, thankless task of cleaning it. I had to recognize that a clean and tidy house is lovely, something I hope to have again someday. But for now I can make it with a somewhat clean and tidy-enough house. And I have to hope my mom won't judge me for it—or if she does, I can overlook it.

I invite you to think of yourself as a movie editor, with five hours of footage more than you need, some scenes that you need to reshoot, some splicing to do between good parts, and some editing/cutting as well. If we enter that editing room and take a good, long look at what we've been taught and what we have not, we can then consider just what kind of mommy movie we want to run for our kids.

H. Norman Wright and Sheryl Wright Macauley say in their book, *Making Peace with Your Mom*:

When there are unresolved issues with Mom, two important factors are at work. One has to do with your feelings for your mother, the hurts you experienced, and the needs she didn't meet. Have you identified these feelings, hurts, unmet needs? The second factor is the dynamics and patterns of relating, which you learned as you interacted with your mom. As you consider these issues, realize that the first one concerns how you feel today about your past and the other deals with how you may be repeating the patterns from your past. *Your future is tied to your past.*[4]

I would imagine that unresolved issues with Dad impact us in similar ways as a parent, but since we're mothers, it's Mom we'll focus on the most here. Our parents, like it or not, probably have a lot to do with the footage we have in hand for our rough-cut of our own parenthood tapes—whether we'd rather leave the whole thing on the cutting room floor and walk away or do a remake of a classic in our own mommy movie. Sometimes, it takes years and the new perspective afforded by parenthood for us to be good film editors.

Women from the survey said:

"I respect them so very much now! I *get* it now!"

Lori

"I appreciate my mom's heart and I am grateful for her help when my children were born. However, I do not want to parent the way she did."

Shellie

"They got a lot smarter, all of a sudden (ha ha!)."

Chelsey

"My parents died before my marriage and children. When my children were very young, I longed for that connection and source of love for our family. Now that they're maxing out preschool, I reflect on parenting and family struggles I witnessed my parents go through, and it gives me a greater perspective and appreciation for where their priorities were."

Andrea

"I see them from a parental point of view. I see how they protected me and raised me while I grew up, and I respect them for many of their decisions as parents."

Beth

All five of these women, who are now parents, are identifying with their parents. That's step one. But read Shellie's quote again. She appreciates her mother and her help but she's clearly identified some things she wants to do differently with her own children. This is a woman who's already been in the film editing room and come out with her own new draft—which will soon be modified after her own field test audience (her children) respond.

Drs. Henry Cloud and John Townsend wrote an excellent book called *The Mom Factor*, one I'd recommend to any mom who wants to think through her childhood and how it is currently affecting her parenting. It's a good basis for this "cutting room/editing room" process.

We need to look at the patterns that we learned in our relationship with our mother. Patterns of avoidance, control, compliance, dominance, passivity, aggressiveness and . . .

mistrust, and a host of others can get hardwired into our brains. We were made to take in those patterns and to live by them. That is what parenting is about. We internalize the ways of our parents, and then live by them. Thus, we are destined to repeat troublesome internalized patterns of relating or performing until we become aware of them and change. In this way, our relationship with mom needs more than forgiveness: We need to become aware of dynamics and patterns and change them into more helpful ones.[5]

Consider Your Parents' Parenting

You have hopes and dreams for your child(ren). I know you do. Every mom does. If you could do this mothering gig thing perfectly, and if the world were more like Eden than the reality we face every day, I bet you'd have a good chance at forming your child into your dream.

We can't control our world, or theirs, but we can lay a good foundation for them. We can try our best, and pray that God's grace will cover us all when we fail. But part of that effort is facing what our family of origin gave us . . . or didn't. We must recognize what was good and bad so that we can break any unhealthy patterns and keep them from echoing in our own family. So consider for a moment how your parent(s):

disciplined	expressed faith
taught	provided security
guided	protected
conveyed love	dealt with frustration
expressed emotion	cheered
corrected behavior	connected
rewarded	empathized
established boundaries	modeled health

. . . or not. How did they succeed? How did they fail? How do you want to do it differently, better?

An important part of this exercise is to discover a measure of grace and understanding for your parent(s). After all, you can't be the peaceful, happy mom you want to be if you're eaten up by bitterness and frustration, right? Often they were only replaying films that had been recorded for them, operating out of a sense of hurt or guilt or shame themselves. So if you're struggling, at some point, try this internal script:

Mom/Dad did the best they could with what they had at the time. I wish it had been different in these ways: _____ _____ but it was what it was. I choose to deal with the potential of the future rather than wallow in the past. I believe that I have been given the freedom to change bad habits and harmful tendencies. Therefore, I will do this with my children: _____ _____ (fill in specifics of what you hope to do). *With God's help, I can!*

My friends and I have wrestled through issues regarding discipline, working/staying at home, faith, guilt, performance/perfectionism, co-dependency, and more. All together, it would give Dr. Phil enough fodder to fuel a year's worth of programs. But it's important to dissect what you were taught (or what you were not) and how much of that you want to pass along to your own children. That's what Jennifer did: "I feel like I am closer to my parents. I can finally understand where they were coming from while I was growing up. I feel like I can also take some of the things that I wish had been different growing up and apply that to my own life (like making my home a little more positive)."

If you're really struggling with issues concerning your mom and dad, or if your mom wasn't there for you or died, and you still haven't processed that impact on your life, I encourage you to read Wright and Macauley's helpful *Making Peace with Your Mom*. It's a really good resource. Or perhaps the issues are so deep and troublesome that you might need a Christian counselor to help you unravel the knot in your

What is the most beneficial thing your parents taught you that you *want* to pass along to your children? Was something emotionally unhealthy conveyed/ ingrained in your mind/heart that you *don't* want to pass along to your children?

stomach; if so, go after it. Remember what Wright said: "Your future is tied to your past." Your future includes your children. It's important to deal with the issues to be the healthiest mom you can be. Listen: we're going to make mistakes. We're all imperfect. But if we know there's something we need to deal with, something that's going to affect our children and our children's children, let's address it, friend. Your future will be so much more enjoyable, fun, and healthy if you're not wallowing in the past.

Now don't hate me, but my parents did a pretty good job with me. They made me feel confident and loved and secure and gave me excellent coping skills. I adopted my mother's clean-house psychosis and a few other negative film clips that I wanted out of my own mothering Blu-ray DVD, but nothing I couldn't deal with. The big puzzle pieces were in place. My parents adore my children and want to spend time with them, giving them what they need too—unconditional love and adoration. Was it perfect? Nah. But it was pretty darn terrific. And in becoming a mom, I enjoyed a new bond with them (and even with my in-laws—*gasp*!).

Judging from our survey, a good number of other people also feel closer to their parents as a result of becoming a parent themselves:

"Our relationship has definitely grown stronger. They actually moved to our town to be here with us to help us when our triplets were eight months old. It has been such a blessing for *all* of us."

Amy

"My mother delights in seeing me experience what she did and laughs with me at my children's antics . . . and then tells me about my own as a child!"

Ali

"Our relationship has definitely improved. They always tell me how proud they are of me as a mom and that I'm doing such a great job."

Anna

"My relationship with my parents improved 100 percent. I totally understand why they were neurotically concerned about what I was doing and whom I was doing it with."

Dana

"We are closer. Although both of our children are adopted, my parents see a lot of me in them and laugh as only parents can when they see history repeating itself!"

Chris

Note, though, that I said "a good number" of people feel closer to their parents after becoming parents themselves.

Others had different experiences. A fair number of women reported that they were estranged from their parent(s) or that their parent(s) had passed on. Others said their parents are still in such an unhealthy state, they can't allow their children near them. One said she'd tried to involve them with her kids, but they really expressed no interest or enjoyment—"they resisted and I gave up."

Girls, if you're a part of this group, I'm sorry for your pain. I'm sorry that you're missing a Grandma or Grampa for your kids or a support for you. Heaven knows, we mothers need some bolstering encouragement—tiny cheerleaders on our kitchen counters shouting, "Gimme an M! Gimme an O! Gimme an M! What does that spell? Hero!"

If this is your experience, may I encourage you to seek out others who might "adopt" you and your children as mentor grandparents? There's a world full of lonely and hurting people out there. I know that there are some older folks who would love to become a part of your lives. Our old neighbors, the Millers, had such a Grandma figure in their lives. She was once a babysitter for them but in time became close enough that they included her at holiday dinners. Is there a neighbor with whom you can strike up a conversation, get to know better? Someone at the community center or your church? Keep your eyes open. God created us as relational beings and he's pretty good about giving us opportunities to relate. Look for people with whom you have something in common and build from there.

Here's how I might reach out to an older person who also seems drawn or open to me: "Hey, I have something

I'd love for you to think over. We're far away/estranged from our extended family and my kids and I are really missing that generation's impact on our lives. Would you be open to coming over for dinner and hanging out with us on Sunday night? We'd love to get to know you better." Open the door, and see what happens.

And what if your parents are around, but you just don't enjoy or connect with them? Nicole said, "Parenting has taken a lot of time away from being with my mom, and she is not happy about it." Marni said, "My parents are not Christians, so they watch us with curiosity as we make decisions based on our Christian beliefs that they don't necessarily understand or approve. My parents are always supportive of us as a family, which is great because my husband's Christian parents have behaved badly toward us—we're no longer even speaking."

Sometimes parents have a hard time dealing with the changes in your life or they might get frustrated that they can't control your family or run your household the way they think is best—but that is their issue not yours. Some might just be jealous for one reason or another. Given time and grace, everyone hopes they will adjust, come around, "see the light." But sometimes they don't. Talk about your boundaries with your husband and agree to support each other in maintaining those boundaries while still reaching out to your parents. Dare to address issues up front with them in a loving manner. And if in time they don't change destructive or negative behaviors, revisit your boundaries and limit your interaction with them. After all, this is your movie, not theirs!

Here's Granny!

One of the big issues that tends to rear its ugly head when you have children is that your parents, particularly the mothers, might expect you to do things the same way they did them. Whether the subject is discipline, feeding schedule, to cuddle them or let them cry themselves to sleep, toilet training, vaccinations, treating a cold, whatever, the typical conversation goes something like this:

> Grandma: "Well, that's an interesting way of handling it. Do you think that's the best way?"
>
> You: "Yes, Hubby and I talked about it and decided this is how we will go about it."
>
> Grandma: "We didn't do it that way."
>
> You: "I know you didn't. But Hubby and I talked about it and decided to do it this way."
>
> Grandma: "Do you think it's wise? Look how well you/ my son turned out. We always thought it was best to do it the other way."

Now that conversation might leave you feeling hurt, angry, disrespected, or doubtful. But remember, Grandma is feeling echoes of love from her life as a young mom and shares some of that intense, no-holds-barred love you feel for your child. She adores her grandchild. Her ultimate goal might feel like control, but she's probably just acting out of love and concern. And she's basing her thoughts on what *did* work for her. Think about how you're eager to inform a girlfriend who's just starting the mommy track about what's worked for you! The goal is just to help her out, hand her a "Get out of jail free" card in Mommy Monopoly, right? Even have time for tea at Park Place! So rather than get all riled up, *assume love and care during this conversation with Grandma,* and then try this:

> You: "Hubby and I read a book/heard this taught/learned about it from a friend, and it really made sense to us. We're trying it this way for now. But tell me a little more about why you think your method worked. I'm open."
>
> Grandma: [Either she'll give you an insightful, thoughtful answer or she might be a little taken aback, having not thought it through for twenty-plus years—or maybe it was just "the way it was done." She might even have to get back to you after she thinks about it. The important thing is to convey respect and yet also *kindly* and *gently* stand your ground.]
>
> You: "Hmm. Well, that makes sense, but I also like how we're going about it now. I'll have to talk about that with Hubby and see what he thinks. [Spread the heat!] But thanks for sharing your thoughts with me. It means a lot that you care so much about our child."

Some parenting methods are cyclical—they're out of fashion for a time and then they're back. You may even decide that Grandma makes sense and opt to leap to her method. But again, assume love, put on an attitude of respect, gently demand respect in return, and you'll get through these conversations in record time . . . and without family trauma.

Out on a Limb: Siblings

I was surprised when my brother Ryan held my firstborn in his big hands, gazing at her with a tender smile, then turned to me and said, "She has our blood running through her veins. The next generation has arrived."

Now Ryan thinks in big-picture, deep-river fashion, so his comment partially took me aback (when others were cooing over her pretty lips or beautiful baby blues), but what also cemented this memory in my head was, at that moment, my brother and I were brought together in a new fashion—and divided. We bonded in those sweet minutes in admiring this next generation of our clan, but also in that moment I felt like I had taken a step further away from him.

I love how he interacts with my kids and they adore their Uncle Ryan. He is basically a kid stuck in massive man-form, so he can identify, play, and discuss things with them on their level. But as a pilot, he can also take them for rides in a private plane. How much cooler can an uncle be? Still, as I married and had children, my life kept evolving in a new area, and I felt that I left him behind and the chasm between us was ever widening.

Women from the survey experienced something similar with their sibs:

"I am less tolerant of my siblings' selfishness and irresponsibility and I let them know it, which causes tension."

Stacie

"My brother and I share parenting stories. We are closer now than we were before. My sister and I are still very close but she does not always understand why I need to be with my family and not on a weekend away with her. She is getting better, though."

Laura

"They don't understand my limitations with things like naps. They feel put out with our special needs."

Denise

We've done our best to keep up with each other's lives over the years. That's probably the key to any relationship after a big life change—to reach back across the chasm and try to engage with people on anything you still have in common, to think about what it might feel like to walk in their shoes.

We tend to become so mama-myopic that we can't get anything else in focus, but we should try not to talk only about life as a mom. "What are you reading? What movies have you seen? What questions have made you think lately?" (I know, I know, it's hard to use your brain when you're weary, but this is important.) Ask questions about your siblings' lives and carve out time after the kids are in bed or napping so you can have an uninterrupted conversation. (*Note*: See pages 61 and 117 for other ideas/discussion starters with friends that can apply here too.)

What would you like your children to gain from interaction with your parents or siblings? How could you best encourage that?

Now Ryan has just married (sixteen years after us), and they hope to have children. Sharing the ups and downs of marital life will be a new bond for us, especially as they have kids. I think it will draw us together even more. I hope I can someday say what Amanda did: "As we've all grown (married and having kids), my three brothers and two sisters and I have only grown closer. We can share experiences and learn from each other (even the black sheep in the family!)."

Not that sharing parenthood is a guarantee for a close-knit relationship:

> "It has been harder for us to get together because of our hectic schedules. We have less time to talk. Our kids are also so different that connecting as families can be difficult."
>
> Tiffany

> "Despite being raised by the same set of parents, my siblings and I have different parenting styles."
>
> Jeri

> "My sister and I have never gotten along, but we have daughters close in age so we get along for them."
>
> Cindy

> "We have less in common than I thought. People get riled up about parenting issues."
>
> Sarah

I hear a good word of caution in these statements—that when and if Ryan becomes a dad, he and his wife might not want to parent like Tim and I have. I can't foist my ways on them (but hopefully they'll recognize the sage wisdom within Ryan's big sister and seek out my advice, as *all* good little brothers must do). But I'll try to keep my mouth shut; I really will. Because he's responsible to lay down the footage for his own children's movies, and I hope to be a part of his children's lives, just as he has been a part of mine.

In the best of worlds, I think greater-clan interaction gives children experience in communication, a sense of stability beyond what we can do on our own (we all love to belong, don't we?), and an understanding of how to deal with even the more difficult people in our lives. Think about it. We can choose to avoid difficult or uncomfortable circumstances almost anywhere else in our lives—we can leave jobs, neighborhoods, churches. But it's harder to leave our families. And maybe God designed it that way for a purpose. By nature we are apt to extend more with "blood relatives"; we love them, so we give them second and third chances and endure irritating tendencies, concentrating instead on the greater good in the picture. This, in essence, is grace in action. We all have our foibles (and make mistakes and have irritating habits); let's strive to treat our family members the same way we'd like to be treated.

Mamas of the Round Table Discussion Questions

1. Talk about your mom and name at least one positive aspect of her parenting that you admire. (Keep this short and sweet; second, related question below.)
2. What are the "movie clips" you wish to integrate into your own children's "emotional/mental movies"—the positive things you gained from your parents? (You can review the list on page 79 to help you think about this.)

3. Has your relationship with a parent ever interfered with your relationship with your husband, as it did for Stephanie in our fiction introduction to this chapter?
4. How has becoming a parent brought your extended family closer together (parents or siblings or both)?
5. What has been the most challenging relationship within your extended family (since you became a parent)? What do you think is the root cause of this difficulty?
6. How important is it that your children know their grandparents? What is special about that relationship?
7. How do your parents interact with your children? Do they ever do anything that bugs you?
8. How do you stay connected to your extended family? If you have separated yourself on purpose, how are you involving others (friends or neighbors) in your child's life?

4

The Club No One Talks about— but Should!

how motherhood changes friendships

I think it's difficult to grow in a friendship if you don't spend time together without the kids. You spend your time together attempting to carry on a conversation but are interrupted so much that it's tough; you also end up comparing yourself and your kids to theirs. Your friendship becomes more about your kids than yourselves.

Cheri

We see each other under challenging conditions and see what we are truly made of. That transparency can make or break a relationship—depending on how gracious and forgiving we are of one another and of ourselves.

Marni

I sooo appreciate my friends' efforts because I know how hard it is. That's why I try to touch base with them every few days to say, "Hey. How are you? No, really—how are you?" and "I care about you. I'm here for you. I love you." The biggest surprise of all? That they do the same thing for me!

Mandi

'm doing it again. Droning on and on about Nina."

"That's okay," Amy said. "Auntie Amy is almost as enthralled with her as her mama."

Jen groaned and fiddled with her glass. "I'm sorry. I don't want to be that lady, that nutso mommy who can't talk about anything but her child."

Amy smiled. "If you think it's bad now, how bad will it be when Amy Two arrives?"

Jen leaned back, trying to take a deep breath. Six weeks to go. Only now was she getting excited over having this baby. But it was mostly so she could eat and sleep again. "I'll try to keep it in check, I promise. And if I don't, just slap me around a little, will you?"

"I'll remind you that you said that. But I can just see myself, getting hauled off by the police for slapping a nursing mother. 'But she told me to slap her!' "

"Okay, that won't go over very well. The world loves pregnant women and nursing mothers. You'd be done for."

Amy took a sip from her glass. "I appreciate your coming out tonight, Jen. I needed someone to talk to."

"It feels good to be out, pal. I'm glad you felt you could reach out to me. I know I haven't been very accessible and I'm guessing you sometimes feel left out of the Fantastic Four when we get together and chat kids and marriage."

"Well, at least I'll get killer hand-me-downs for my kiddos, when and if I ever meet Mr. Dreamy. But right now, that's feeling like a long shot."

Jen leaned forward. "What are you talking about? You're beautiful, smart, and you already own your own condo and car. You're funny and—"

"Jen, I found a lump."

Jennifer paused and tried to gather her thoughts. *A lump? In her breast?* "What are you talking about? You're thirty years old."

"It's cancerous."

"Oh, no." Her mind whipped in a hundred different directions. Amy's grandmother had died of breast cancer, she remembered, but she had been old. Old, right? They had been ten, maybe twelve, making her grandmother at least fifty or sixty. "They can treat it, right? You have options?"

"I got tested last year for the gene. You know, the cancer gene? My mom has already had a bout of cancer, a mastectomy, remember? And my grandmother . . ."

"I remember," Jen said, reaching across the table to take her hand.

"It was positive. This thing is coming for me." Amy moved her hand away and wrapped it around her glass instead. She took a swig, as if steeling herself. "I'm going to have them removed."

"Have what removed?"

"My breasts."

Jennifer stared at her friend. She had meant it when she said Amy was beautiful; she was a hottie, always had been. She had one of those long, lithe bodies, accentuated by platinum blonde hair, and hips and breasts that begged to be dressed in '60s slim. Even now, two college boys were looking in their direction, and it wasn't Jen's cute preggers belly that was drawing their attention.

"Say something, Jen."

"I . . . I'm uh . . . I'm trying to get my mind around what you're saying, Ames. My best friend just told me not only that she has cancer but she's thinking about undergoing a life-altering surgery. Gimme a sec to absorb all that."

Amy raised an eyebrow but then focused on her soda, swirling it around in her glass, before finishing it off. A minute later a waitress brought another soda. "Courtesy of the boys over there," she said.

"Tell them thanks, but they'd better keep to the college co-eds," Amy said with a sweet smile. She raised her glass in the young men's direction and then turned back to Jen. Jen couldn't remember the last time a man, other than Alex, had looked her way, let alone thought about buying her a drink.

"So what you're saying is you're scared, so scared you think you need to take off your breasts."

"That scared, yes."

"What'd they say about the lump? Have they removed it?"

"Aspirated. The news came back this morning that it's cancerous."

"And so your doctor recommended this?"

"He recommended a partial mastectomy. If he'd recommended a lumpectomy, I'd think twice. But if he's scared enough to say mastectomy, I say go twice as far. And take 'em both while you're at it. I'm not going to go the route of my grandmother."

"Slow down there, Cujo," Jen said. "I think one should pause before she casts off body parts."

Amy smiled and fiddled with her napkin. "I need you to think it through with me, Jen. Pros and cons. You've always been good at that."

"Okay . . . Pros. You get rid of the cancer and limit chances of a return, right?"

"Limit but not eradicate. However, the less flesh there is to inhabit, the less chance a bad neighbor moves in next door."

"Got it. Back to pros: peace of mind?"

"Yes. At least, as much as you can, once cancer's been in your bod."

Jen pulled out a piece of paper and scribbled some notes. "Okay, cons. Go."

"Radical surgery. A piece of my body, literally gone. Fake stuff in its place."

Jen glanced up at her. "Reconstruction?"

"Yeah, they can do it right away. I mean, if I want."

"If you want," Jen said with a nod, and wrote it down.

"And then there's men. What if my dream man can't handle it? Can't handle that my breasts are . . . you know . . . not mine?"

"They'd be yours, Ames. And your dream man wouldn't be that shallow. Right? Unless you've revised the model we've been perfecting since we were twelve years old."

"No, I haven't. So that's a pro, right? It would help me filter out the serious Dreamsters from the Nightmares super fast. I could just introduce myself with that key information. 'Hi, I'm Amy McCallister and I've had a double mastectomy and major reconstruction. Does that put you off?'"

Jen laughed with her. "Yeah, I'd call that a pro—helps you get down to brass tacks with Mr. Potential Dreamy." She looked up from her sheet of paper. "What else?"

Amy thought for a moment. "No breast-feeding. You know, if I'm ever blessed enough to have a child."

"Lots of babies out there do just fine on bottles, Ames."

"I know. It's just the idea that it's not my choice anymore."

"But you can have kids. You know . . . after?"

"After I'm cancer-free for a while. But I assume Mr. Dreamy won't emerge for a bit, so that's okay. I still have time to get well and get preggers."

"And you'd have a better chance at that? Being cancer-free, I mean?"

"Yeah. It's not in my lymph nodes, at least from what they can tell. And that's a good sign." She slid her glass away from her. "Would you come, Jen? If I have it? Would you come for the surgery?"

Her plaintive tone made Jen want to cry. Most of Amy's family were gone; her mother and father were down in the Sun Belt, but even further away emotionally.

"You know I'll be there. Maybe I can come and be with you for the surgery, and then just slide down the hall to have this baby. They could wheel you down so you could coach me through labor. Alex isn't the best at that. You—even drugged up—would be better."

Amy smiled. "I could do that. And we could spare Alex fainting again. He could just hang out in the waiting room like our grandfathers did and come in for the moment of glory."

"Sounds like a plan to me. Come on. Let's go to the car and pray for a bit. I think you need some guidance on your decision from God, not me. I'm with you, whatever you decide. But let's ask him to show you what's best, okay?"

"Okay. Thanks for being there for me, Jen."

"Any time," she said, looping an arm around Amy's waist. "And I'm not ready to give you up yet, got it? You have to beat this cancer deal. It can't have you. I couldn't handle losing you."

"Unless it's to the future Mr. Dreamy."

"Yeah, okay. I'll make room for him when he arrives on his white horse, but not this dragon. This monster is going to get a sword in the belly. We're going to fight back."

Welcome to the Club

My mom has always said that it was easiest to find friends when she was a young mom, and we (her kids) were in school. This gave her instant access to a world of women with whom she immediately had something in common—motherhood! It's so natural, sometimes it sneaks up on us. Jennifer said, "My friends now all have children. I find my children's friendships creating relationships for me." It's almost supernatural—that village-builder of shared motherhood! Sharyl said, "Once you become a mom, you unofficially enter the 'mommy club' and you bond with other moms whom you may or may not have had a bond with before."

> "I don't have any non-mom friends anymore! Where'd they go?"
>
> *Beth Ann*

It wasn't instantaneous for me. When I first became a mom, Tim and I lived in a teeny tiny town, heavily populated by retirees, and we belonged to a church where we were the youngest by fifteen years. I worked with many people, but many of their children were older than ours. Elsewhere my best friends from high school and college were just getting married, and children were nothing but a future plan.

It was only when we moved to Colorado and joined a larger church filled with young families that I caught a glimpse of what my mom had been talking about. There's something about going belly to belly with another preggers female or finding out your children were born in the same month (or even the same year) that instantly ties you together. Quickly we found our place within a social group, all sharing children about the same age, and it was so fun!

We got together constantly—to celebrate the children's birthdays at Chuck E. Cheese (man, we hated that place, but the kids adored it!), Halloween trick-or-treating, Christmas family parties, July 4th. And the moms would often leave the kids at home with Dad to go to one another's home parties and a chance to have adult conversation; we did everything, leaping at the opportunity to be "just girls"—Partylite, Pampered Chef, Princess House, Weekenders, Christmas Around the World, jewelry shows, stamping shows, art shows (I'm serious, *everything*! It was a major coup when someone discovered an untried show). We met at the park for playdates, celebrated Mom birthdays, and together launched a MOPS program at church.

> "I'm closer to friends with kids because we have much more in common. It's like going to a female GYN—the doctor knows what you're talking about!"
>
> *Victoria*

Those were sweet, tender, exploratory years. We moms were just figuring out what it meant to be a mom, how to discipline, how to protect, how to let go, how to love, how to mold a child into a decent human being. Best of all, we were a support to one another, sharing recipes but also instantly on hand in a crisis. Not being alone—having others around me who really understood what it was like—is something I'll always treasure, a gift from God.

The Change (No, Not *That* One)

But those friendships were *new* friendships for me. In the survey, nearly three-quarters of respondents saw a change in their friendships after they landed on Planet Mom—with moms and non-moms alike. Like marriage or a move, it seems that motherhood is a dividing point for many friendships, especially if you were the first one to step into this brave, new world. It makes sense—any big change in a life can either bring people together or shove them apart. Just because you are madly in love with the most perfect, precious baby in the world doesn't mean your friend won't see him as anything more than a poopster who makes your whole house smell bad or a writhing, screaming mass of flesh who seems to interrupt every decent, meaningful conversation you have. Just as she may have once been jealous of your falling in love with a man and spending all your time with him, now she has to adjust to your time and energy being even more limited.

And though fellow moms will welcome you into the aforementioned club, since there is an instant bond in place because you "get" one another, there still might be disagreements on how you raise your child, developmental comparisons that get under your skin, or varying disciplinary standards that make it seem impossible to spend time together. Just because you're both moms doesn't mean you are going to be BFFs. You still have to like and respect each other as individuals.

Women from the survey noted a thread of competition among fellow moms (one said to a Survey Mom: "You're not truly a stay-at-home mom until you have two children, since one is still portable"!), comparison of children's successes and gifting, kids not getting along, disagreement about discipline strategies, and more. Amy said, "I am finding moms in general are real busy staying busy. Most moms do not have time just to relax and enjoy life, [let alone a real friendship]. They just don't know how to do that. They spend all their energy living up to the world's social standards—having 'Johnny' in this and 'Janey' in that and being involved in every social club themselves to boot—instead of living up to their own standards."

When asked what *good* friendships with fellow moms give them, the respondents answered with some of the following phrases:

mutual understanding	funny stories
connection	compassion
frank, open conversation	empathy
shared experiences	commiseration
trusted advice	camaraderie
deeper bond	respect
shared priorities	support
	mentoring

But even if you love the new mommy club you were initiated into the instant your child urped all over your favorite party dress or exploded through her diaper, covering the whole crib in poop, or coughed like a seal, forcing you to stand in a hot, steamy bathroom at two in the morning, the club isn't enough to keep all young mothers together. To create lasting, deep friendships, time, effort, shared priorities, grace, and devotion are needed.

Mommy's Time Out

You may not feel that you can stay awake later than eight o'clock these days, but it really is important to grab some time, after the kids are asleep (or during their naps), to reach out to your friends. Better yet, arrange to put the kids down and then leave them with your husband or a sitter while you join your pal at the corner coffeehouse for a decaf and catch-up time. I see so many mommies who are never without children in tow, as if they are not small individuals but rather new appendages growing from their hip. I understand the impulse—we want to provide for and connect with and nurture our children— but we, and our friendships, need time sans child too. (If this advice is freaking you out, remember, you can leave them with Dad or a babysitter *after they are asleep*! They'll never know you're gone!) Trust me on this. If friendship—having a real heart-friend—is important to you, hang out together and include the child some of the time, but other times, leave your child at home and go out on your own. *When you became a mom, you did not cease being an individual.*

> "Time [with friends but including children] is often compromised by the needs of the children. Can we at least finish one sentence?"
>
> *Melissa*

This allows two friends to actually finish a conversation. When you have children, especially young children, it's often difficult to find the time and space to have a conversation that (a) doesn't revolve around children or (b) dares to go to a deeper place. You can do this in a mere 1.5 hours away from home—20 minutes to drive to/from, 10 minutes to order coffee, 20 minutes of catch-up time, and 40 minutes of heart-to-heart. Surely your hubby or a friend can mind the fort with a sleeping child for an hour and a half! Or during the "blessed, quiet hours" at home, instead of tuning in to a TV show, tune in to your friend. Make a phone date to catch up, even if it's with a pal who lives nearby.

"A" for Effort

Listen, I know what it's like to be so darn tired that picking up the phone feels equivalent to picking up an elephant. There is a time and place for everything. If you're not missing your friends, if your highest priority is simply stringing together five hours of decent REM sleep, if you're in survival/newborn mode, this might not be the time. Real friendships take effort. Real friendships also will last through a season of relative distance. Just do *what* you can *when* you can.

But when you've raised your head up and realized you need to laugh with a friend, watch and discuss a movie, read a book and wrestle with a question the author has raised, hang out with anyone who has a vocabulary greater than a hundred words, seek advice about marriage or parenthood or faith or politics, that just might be your cue to start your trek toward Real Friendship Peak.

Granted, when we're running around like chickens with our heads cut off, it's hard to focus on the friend in front of us or the friend we have yet to meet, but effort is often rewarded by success. Coming off an Olympics year, sports are on my mind. Given an even talent pool, the most gifted athletes are those who push, risk, and *work at it* the most.

Time magazine concurs: "Rather than mere experience or even raw talent, it is dedicated, slogging, generally solitary exertion—repeatedly practicing the most difficult physical tasks for an athlete, repeatedly performing new and highly intricate computations for a mathematician—that leads to first-rate performance."[6]

The correlation is that friendship, the real, heartfelt, until-we-die friendship I believe every woman craves, takes work to unearth and build. "First-rate performance," translated to a friendship realm, means finding someone you trust, love, celebrate, and enjoy. "The most difficult physical tasks," translated to friendship, means spending time together or being there for her when she needs you, even if you have equal or greater needs. "Highly intricate computations" translates to serious, heartfelt, meaningful conversation.

The really good news in that report on achieving success is that effort can supersede raw talent or experience in making friends; even if you've never had a true friend before, even if you've failed in the past, you can succeed now. You just have to try, again and again. *Try*.

Shared Priorities

If you are looking for a heart-friend-to-be, you are likely to find her in communities that you enjoy and that meet some need. Church, schools, a sports club, and neighborhood gatherings are good places to start. The idea is not to share just motherhood but other interests as well. Where would you look for a friend if you were not a mom? Maybe it's a volunteer organization. What are you passionate about?

What's important to instill in your children? Which organizations will help you do that? Invariably, this is a good place to *start*.

For me, faith, family, and balanced living are my top three priorities in life. I'm a

Do you have that woman who embodies trust, love, celebration, and enjoyment in your life? If so, how are you investing in your relationship? If not, how will you take a step forward in finding her?

mom who limits her children's activities because God and family always come first. Over the years this commitment has separated me from some early "club friends" but drawn me closer to a precious few who see things the way I do (or will challenge me if I'm off base), support my values, care about every member of my family, and encourage me to be all my God has created me to be. Because faith is my number one priority, I've found women in places like church, Bible study, and Christian work who became good friends. A couple of them do not have children. One has older children. Others have younger children. So in the end, being a mommy in the same stage of life was something that brought me together with many, but it was *shared priorities* that narrowed the group down to those who mean the most to me.

Grace and Devotion

Along with shared priorities, there are important qualities that have helped me build for-life friendships. My heart-friends offer grace to cover my failures—and I do the same for them. We share a devotion and a genuine care and empathy for each other.

To be sure, I've failed my friends time and time again. Over the years I'm sure each could point to times I've been judgmental, shrill, irritable, unkind, lackadaisical, uncaring, delusional, bossy, unfeeling, nosy, headstrong, and rude. Fortunately two things have saved our friendships: I'm not all bad all the time, and grace abounds.

Now *grace* might be a word you're not familiar with. I'm not speaking of the grace we say before a meal. In Christian culture we use the word most often when referring to how Jesus's sacrifice covers all the sins we have committed and will commit in the future. In short, his perfection fills in the gaping holes our sinful imperfections create. God's grace is unearned but still freely given.

In an echo of that gift, good friends offer grace to their friends. Grace in friendship is like my kids' Silly Putty, able to fit in tiny crevices or, if needed, a harrowing, deep crevasse. True friends understand that we will fail them, but all humans fail. The goal is to pick ourselves up and strive to do better next time.

Dee Brestin writes:

When a friend lets us down, we show that our theology [or thinking] is off base when we're overcome with shock. The Bible teaches that we're all going to let each other down. Even the most beautiful rose has thorns. Preaching professor at Trinity Evangelical Seminary, Greg Scharf,

Circle your three top priorities:
Emotional health • Mental growth • Social connection • Health/exercise • Faith • Balance • Politics • Finances • Education • Environment • Marriage • Family life • Friendship • Other:_____ • Other: _____

Where would be good places to meet other women with similar priorities?

says, "When someone fails you, don't be stunned! It's more appropriate to think, *Hmmmm! That confirms what Scripture teaches—that we're all sinners, that there's none that is righteous, no, not one.*"[7]

A favorite radio host, Dennis Prager, obviously would agree with Brestin. He has been known to say, "Expectations lead to unhappiness." Now I hope my friends will treat me with love and respect, that I can count on them in an emergency, that they will consider my children dear to them, but Prager is right. If I don't extend some grace, allow them to fail the subliminal expectations hovering about my heart like a thin fog, then I will be unhappy and disappointed.

Now friends, true friends, if they share your priorities and are treating you well and not going through a crisis themselves, will characteristically be there for you.

If you have no one in your life whom you admire, no one who inspires you to be more than you are now, no one encouraging you to grow in all the important ways—love,

> The finest friends in life are those you admire, people you want to become *more like* as you mature.

joy, peace, grace—then you need to add a new friend to your group!

While we grant those we love and admire a measure of grace for when they fail to meet our expectations, we have to make certain that our investment in the relationship is worthwhile. Dee Brestin likens friends to either roses—all of which have thorns that can occasionally scratch, poke, or even draw blood—or alligators, who have long snouts filled with jagged teeth that can rip you apart.[8]

If your friendship is one-directional (always about her, never about you, even in the good times) or revolving around jealousy or sniping or centering on the dark side of life—or anything else negative you'd prefer to have out of your life—it might be time to step away from that friend. But before you do, I urge you to try to encourage your friend to grow—remember love, joy, and peace?—with specific changes you'd like to see in the friendship.

We all get into certain habits and routines with certain friends. Habits and routines take effort to redirect. Begin by deciphering what, exactly, is bothering you about your friendship. For instance, I'm the planner (I love planning), but lately I feel as though I'm always the one who has to arrange the dates with our best couple friends. It feels like I'm begging for time, and if it's important to them to be together, they could take the initiative.

So last week, when I asked about when we could get together again, and my BFF said, "I'll have to get back to you on that," I said, "That's fine. I'll consider the ball in your court now." I'm not going to chase it anymore. She'll call, in time. It might take longer than I'd like for us to get together, but I won't feel irritated or frustrated that I always have to chase down the date, time, and place. Resolution! I love that.

Friends without the Secret Password *(Psst . . . It's "Baby")*

And then there are those friends, left outside the clubhouse, without the secret password to enter. You stare out of the window, wistfully wishing they could follow you in, but there is an initiation fee, payable only via your health insurance deductible after labor and delivery or the adoption agency's countless fees. That's club rule number one: you must have a child of your own.

This frequently leaves us at odds with our old pals. Survey respondents said:

"Several have stopped talking to me all together."

"My non-mom friends have a hard time relating to me now."

"They just don't get it."

"They don't understand my devotion to my family."

Other moms noted that it wasn't just single friends who were miffed they couldn't go out and party or be available to them at the drop of a hat anymore. It was also married friends who were struggling with infertility. When things shift in a friendship on a seismic scale (such as marriage or children or divorce), it makes sense that there will be a period of adjustment. If some buildings got toppled during the seismic shock (think earthquake), then there might be some rebuilding to be done.

Who is your best friend? Is there anything you feel needs to be addressed with her to clear the way for a deepened or continued friendship? Write down some things you might say to her.

Writing it down is a good exercise—you can get rid of the excess anger and frustration and edit down your thoughts to bare facts and clearly defined needs. A page of spewing might become two sentences of tight, clear, helpful discussion starters to get you on the right track and help you define what you should not say. Then be sure to leave it for a day or two; think and pray about it before you have an actual conversation. Time and sleep are two of the greatest editors in life!

Friendship Off Track?
Healthy "Redirection" Scripts to Practice

Here are some ways I'd hope my BFF would talk to me, encourage me, if I were wandering too deeply or too long in one of these unhealthy "roles."

The "Burdened": (After you've listened to her struggle for a while.) "That's a lot to shoulder. I'm so sorry it's so hard, but life can't be all bad, can it? Tell me about some of the *good* things that are happening for you right now."

The "Teaser": (After a jab that is disguised as "teasing.") "I can see why you'd make fun of me for that. I know I usually laugh at myself for that too, but I have to let you know that it hurts my feelings a bit. Is there something beneath it, deep down, we need to discuss?"

The "Whiner": "I know life is hard and I want you to know I'm here for you. But I'd really like it if we could focus our conversations on how we get past the struggles, how we want to grow, heal, be happy in life. I want to focus on taking steps *forward* in life. Are you game to try to see life like that with me?"

The "Dictator": "I realize you usually pick the place we meet, but there's a cute little restaurant on the west side I've wanted to try. Let's meet there next time, okay?"

The "Oblivious": "Hey, I've been needing to discuss something big with someone. Do you have some time today or tomorrow to listen to me and help me sort it out?"

The "Sniper": "You probably didn't mean to be unkind, but things like what you just said hurt me. I'd really appreciate it if you didn't say it again. I love you, and I want our friendship to grow."

The "User": "I love that you feel you can rely on me and I want to be here for you. Lately I've been feeling like I could use a little lift myself. I was wondering if you could . . ."

For those friends you wish to hold on to, for the friendships that really count, consider talking to your friend about it. You might say: "Things have changed for us since I had the baby. I know it must be frustrating trying to deal with me and my new life. But I want you to know you're important to me, and I'd like to be friends forever. What do you think this new phase of our friendship might look like?" If the two of you can rebuild together, it's bound to be a stronger, more stable relationship. Just be open, honest, and straightforward. You'll avoid a ton of hurt feelings.

Many of the survey respondents commented on the struggle with non-mom friends:

"Some friends without kids don't 'get' what it means to be a mom. They don't understand the time and commitment it is but also don't see what a true joy it is."

Lynette

"Until you are there (are a mom) it is difficult to understand how that really changes your life. We don't talk as much because there is less time to do so."

Sarah

"Once you become a mom, your priorities change, and non-moms can't relate to that. You can still be friends, of course, but things that were once important to you and still are to them, just aren't that important anymore. Life changes."

Ann

"It's harder to talk to them because all I want to talk about, or all I really know anymore, are my child and parenting strategies."

Jean

113

"The priorities that occupy my time and energy make my routine look so much different than theirs or than it used to. I realize how much I was an emotional support and listening ear for them, and my family now gets my best efforts and energies, not the leftovers."

Andrea

"It's hard for them to understand. Plus, I don't want my children to discourage them from having kids if they are misbehaving or something."

Teresa

"Some non-mom friends I used to have quit spending time with me because they could not relate to my situation. I only hope that when they do have children, they will realize what a benefit it was to have non-mom friends, friends you could talk to about things other than spit-up and poop."

Courtney

"Non-moms have really shied away from our friendship. I can't go out every night at a drop of a hat and don't like to party because of the responsibilities I have with my children and husband. I got boring."

Rauscha

"I tend to get upset when friends who work full-time but don't have children assume that since I stay home during the day with my kids, I must have all the free time in the world. I get defensive about my choice to stay home."

Carody

"I feel guilty talking about my daughter or day when chatting with friends who want to be married with kids."

Danielle

These responses reveal that division in a friendship can come from many different angles. Wherever the problem is originating, see if you can address it with your friend. Try discussing it gently but forthrightly, clearly, lovingly. Note what has changed and what has not.

Sometimes you may feel just a tad envious of your non-mom friend. Maybe you're fantasizing about time to yourself, an uninterrupted night's sleep, eating out at a nice restaurant. It's important to recognize these reactions on your part and deal with them honestly. One survey respondent said, "We are still friends, but I struggle to talk to her now because I'm all wrapped up in what the kids are doing. She tells me about her travels and the books she's read, and I can only talk about the book I have memorized, *Goodnight Moon*. I dream of dinner with my husband, let alone a ten-day cruise. It's hard to find a connection that doesn't make her sad or make me a little envious of her freedoms."

I hear that. When I was a younger mom, I'd have days that I wished no one would talk to me or call out for me or touch me. I wanted the day to be solely about me. I wanted to escape for a day and adopt my "free" friends' lives for twenty-four hours.

So for friendships that you want to keep, those sisters-of-the-heart you hope to be in rockers on the porch with when you're old, it's worth the effort to try to find the ways to bridge the gap that having children can cause.

Some friends may get married and become mothers, and this may bring you closer in a later season. Some friends may remain single but will still be fascinating, inspiring, and supportive people in your life. Consider the woman as an individual—regardless of the relationships she has or doesn't have. Is she kind, funny, adventurous, thoughtful, smart, caring, engaging, interesting, interested, a conversationalist, a learner, loving, supportive, growing, healthy, inspiring, sweet, the kind of person you love? Any one of these qualities is a good spark beneath friendship kindling. Three or more could build a nice, warm fire.

So put yourself in that non-mom's shoes. Be empathetic and caring. Consider how you might love her and nurture your friendship. Treat her as an equal. Reach out to her and her current reality and help her find the way to identify with you too.

Support her, just as you hope she'll support you. Talk about how you want to remain friends, and what's realistic for both of you, given your new situation (time, energy, focus). Make plans to talk or get together once a month, without the children. Bring her into your child's life (but not just as a babysitter!); invite her to join you for a family evening or a lazy Saturday to just hang out. Remember, you're fashioning new bridges over a new river. If it's important, you'll start pouring cement into the bulwarks!

Other ways survey respondents helped bridge the non-mom friendship gap:

touching base via email
making spontaneous calls
holiday get-togethers
walking together
focusing on common interests
praying together
seeing chick flicks husbands don't care about

going to restaurants without kids or video games

volunteering together for an organization of mutual interest

having conversations that don't center on my beautiful, talented, funny, clever children

A Word about Cliques

Okay, high school is behind us, *far* behind some of us! I know that it's tempting, once you find that social circle of pals, to just stick with them, but may I encourage you to be always looking outward? Two of my best friends— heart-friends that will be with me until I'm old—are two I would have never been drawn to right away. In fact initial impressions on both fronts were pretty negative, and it was only because I was in a college class with one (and learned in time that she was smart and funny and caring) and I worked with the other (whom I discovered was clever and wise and tender) that I almost missed two sisters who have changed my life. One is not married. The other has

---

Conversation Starters with Non-mom Friends:

"How do you think you would handle this situation?"

"Tell me about your day. I want to visualize you at work. What fills your work hours? What do you like best? What do you loathe?"

"Tell me about your other friends these days. What draws you together?"

"You can probably guess my greatest challenge these days. What's yours?"

no children, but they are both dear to me and my life would have been less fulfilling without them in it.

Experience with these two girls has taught me to always look beyond, look deeper, give time to those around me whom I wouldn't at first peg as girlfriend material. I know I just told you to look for BFFs among those who share your priorities, your passions, and your ideals, but not *every* friend has to be in the exact same niche, right? Finding unique women outside of your normal girlfriend pool will push you to grow—it will challenge you, teach you, encourage you, broaden you and your world. In my girlfriend pool, I have the friend I pray with, the friend I strategize with, the friend who makes me work out, the friend who makes me laugh, the friend I could spend days with, the friend I love to be with for a couple of hours and then I'm spent—you get the picture. They're all different women. Some wouldn't even mix well together, but that's okay, I just keep them apart! And collectively, they feed different aspects of my personality and life.

Please, please, please, give everyone a shot. Better yet, give them three. Wouldn't you want to be given the same?

A Field of . . . Change?

Relationships, all relationships, evolve and change, just as we do. There will be friends you wish to keep and others you need to part with, even if it's just for a season. Your parting might make you feel wistful and sad for a time, or you might try to keep the triumph out of your voice when you say (in so many words), "Don't let the door hit you on the rear!" All of it is okay because there are more friends ahead of you, and your time is finite. You can only do so much, so determine what you want your friendship field to look like and then start casting seeds. The harvest will far outweigh the effort you put into it.

Are you clique focused? How would you feel if you were on the outside, wishing to take part? Are you open to inviting others outside your group to come in? How do you do that now or how will you do that in the future? Are you willing, deep down, truly willing, to give people who don't pass your initial review one more chance (and another and another)?

Mamas of the Round Table Discussion Questions

1. Do you have a best friend or numerous best friends? Where did you find them and how did each relationship become a heartfelt, long-term friendship?
2. Have you ever hurt a friend (or has she hurt you) in a significant way? How did you get past that?
3. Have you ever had a one-directional friend—someone who expects the friendship to be all about her? If so, did you confront her about it? What changed? Or did it end the friendship?
4. What are your friendships with non-moms like? How do you make them work?
5. How many friends do you think you need to feel satisfied on this relationship front?
6. Do you intend to seek out and forge new friendships? How will you do so?

5

Globa-Mama

how becoming a mom changes your relationship with the world

My worldview has softened. Compassion for all people has increased. Protection of my family is my priority.

Lisa

I see the world as a place in desperate need of strong, kind, positive individuals who truly want to make it a better place. My purpose is to raise my kids to be those individuals.

Jenny

Now most material wants seem trivial! My highest dream is peace, health, happiness for my kids and the world.

Julie

Being a mom makes me see a lot more of the "bad" part of the world and wonder what it will be like for my kids when they are my age. But it also makes me see more of the "good" part of the world and see some of the things that have gotten better since when I was little.

Gail

L et me out of this wheelchair," Jen said, staring back at Keisha. "I want to go into labor. This child was due three days ago. Walking might get me going."

"I thought you still weren't ready to be a mother of two," Keisha said.

"That was yesterday. Today I just want this child out."

"Well, you can go into labor after the Fantastic Four finish this race," Keisha said, her typical bossy self. "Sit down!"

Jen sighed and met Amy's amused glance. "If I have to be in a chair," she said, "it's only fair that you do too." Three weeks since her surgery, and she looked pale, but as beautiful and perfect as ever. Stephanie was pushing her wheelchair in this 5K Race for the Cure mini-marathon, just as Keisha was manning Jen's.

Jen watched as Mike came up and gave Stephanie a kiss on the cheek, with Spencer at his side and Ian on his back. It was good to see the four of them back together, a family again. And from all reports, it sounded like things were back on track for them all. Even Steph's mother was in a better place, reportedly off to Iceland with her friend. Something about a blue lagoon and hot springs amidst vast ice fields . . .

"Five minutes and counting," came a voice over the loudspeaker.

"This means a lot, you guys," Amy said, "that you'd all be here, be willing to race for my cause."

"This is our cause too now," Stephanie said, reaching down to touch Amy's shoulder.

"Yeah, the Fantastic Three just doesn't have the same ring to it," Keisha said.

Jen just reached out and held Amy's hand for a minute. "It's cool to be sharing in this, fighting for a cause together, and with people across the country and beyond."

"Fighting back against the dragon?" Amy said.

"You know it. Our swords are drawn, Sistah," Jen said. "He can just stay in his cage and away from you."

"Yeah, he might've gotten a nibble but he can't have any more tasty morsels, not while we're around," Stephanie added.

"That's what I'm talkin' about," Keisha said. "We really oughta have our own TV show. But for now, let's race. After we win this, we'll figure out what else we can do to take down the dragon. Not only do we Fantastic Four have bodies for running—"

"Walking," Steph said with a tone of warning. "You said we could walk most of it, Keish—"

"Bodies made for walking, with some running, but we also have brains. Let's put 'em together and come up with our own plan to help fund some cancer research."

"I like it," Amy said, looking around at them all, tears in her eyes. "I like all of you so much. In fact I believe I love you all."

"Love you too, Ames." Keisha said. "Now let's not embarrass ourselves in this race. Let's at least start running, Stephanie, at least in front of our men."

"Okay," Steph said, smiling over at her husband. "I'd love to watch his face. He'd be shocked to see me tear out of here, running. But just until we're around that bend. Got it?"

"Got it," Keisha said.

"And somewhere along the way, I get to get out and walk," Jen said.

"Na-uh. You're staying in that seat until you can see the finish line. We're not getting disqualified on some flimsy excuse such as labor. We're registered as a team. I'll see my teammate to the finish line or die trying."

"I believe she means it," Amy said, one brow raised.

"There's no arguing with her, once she's like this," Steph put in.

"Fine," Jen said. "But once that finish line is in sight, I'm walking beside my teammate over it."

"Oh!" Amy said. "And I will too! We'll be like a made-for-TV movie! The pregnant lady, the cancer survivor, and their best friends seeing them both through. I'm already teary!"

"I like it," Keisha said, putting her hand down between them. The other three piled their hands on top of hers in silent agreement. "Now let's show these people what the Fantastic Four can do, shall we?"

I know how it is here on Planet Mom. It's sometimes hard to think any further than tonight's dinner (and whether you have all the groceries to fix it). Buried in the day-to-day, we fall behind on keeping in touch with our friends and extended family, let alone staying up to date on community events (unless it involves our children). And beyond our local community, national and world events and changes can seem daunting and overwhelming. Sometimes we choose to turn off the news and the radio and the Internet, incapable of dealing with Earth's six billion people, any number of whom might be going through pain and suffering and struggle. We numb ourselves with sweet books and mindless magazines/TV because that is all we can handle. And that is fine for a season. Sometimes, just to cope, we need a season of neutrality and peace.

But deep down, something has changed in your heart. When you are strong enough to endure it, you turn the TV back on and listen to the news. You find it inspiring, that young mother's story, about how she's trying to raise money to fund her daughter's cancer therapy. You are moved by reports of a drought in Africa and pictures of mothers unable to feed their babies because they are malnourished and dehydrated. It infuriates you to hear of young girls being raped by gangs. You get a lump in your throat when you watch a mother cradle her blood-soaked, unconscious child on a war-ravaged street. It makes your knees shake when you hear of hundreds of schoolchildren crushed in an earthquake, and their mothers' cries reverberate through your chest as if you were *right there*.

You *are* right there, in a sense. Becoming a mom has connected you to mothers throughout your immediate community and indeed all around the world. If you met another mother in a far-off country and couldn't speak a word of the other's language, if you each knew the other was a mother, you would know a lot about each other. You would know this other mother loves fiercely, protects vigilantly, cares selflessly, and dreams with steadfast hope. Motherhood brings out all these fine things in each of us—in greater measure in some than others—but I contend we all exhibit these beautiful attributes in the act of mothering.

We also all strive to create an environment in which our children will thrive. We want to provide for them not just decent food and water but good sleep, healthy playtime, connection with others, and education, and you realize that every day you and your family are making an impact on your children, forming them, bit by tiny bit, just as a mother in Japan is doing the same. Anna said, "I am leaving a footprint in the minds of our girls with every decision I make. I want them to learn by seeing not by just hearing. If my husband and I are conscientious in our decisions, they will be also. Whether that is praying, recycling, choosing organic foods, wearing a seat-belt or bike helmet, being nice to animals, being gracious and polite, they will be more apt to do it if we are doing it first."

We impact our children in a big way, and they, us. And so our first community is our immediate family. Our second is friends and extended family. Our third has a specific, defined place where we are regularly drawn together to meet—such as a church or a school or a moms' support group—with a joint cause. Our fourth is our "neighborhood," which might be our building or floor or maybe an entire town, depending on how rural or urban we are. I'd put online communities in this pocket too, since they have similar attributes. Our fifth is our nation, especially if we anticipate raising our children to adulthood here. And our sixth "community" is the broader world.

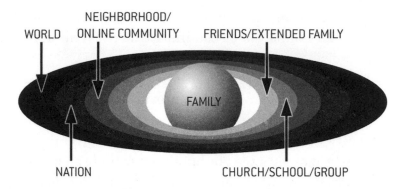

WORLD   NEIGHBORHOOD/ONLINE COMMUNITY   FRIENDS/EXTENDED FAMILY

FAMILY

NATION   CHURCH/SCHOOL/GROUP

That is how I've segmented my "Planet Mom Community Pockets." The core is your precious family. That's where you start, where you live, day to day. But eventually, when you emerge from momnesia, you remember that you love other people too and you need to reconnect with them. So you reach out to that second ring. And you keep on reaching out, connecting with each of those community pockets or rings (with some, over the course of months; with others, over the course of years) because you've realized that this is not just your world, it's your child's too.

There is an aha moment in each mama's life when she comes to understand that what is happening now will affect her child and her child's child. So it's not just a change in awareness of how we are all entwined on earth—it's also a change in awareness that *we are making personal history*. Now. The choices we make today, the battles we wage, the causes

> Take a look at the graphic above. How far are you reaching out to the world? What is your involvement in each ring? Is that okay with you for now or do you feel moved to venture a little further out?

we champion, the lines we hold, the misconceptions we rectify, the injustices we right, the problems we solve—all of it will echo twenty years down the line—and fifty—and a hundred.

Whew. That's big, isn't it? And trust me, I'm no social activist. I'm ashamed to admit that I use paper towels and drive gas hog vehicles (we're saving for a good mileage vehicle because of fuel prices). But that's because my personal causes are more on the faith level, the heart level, than the environmental level *because that's what lights my torch.* But I believe God instills different passions within each of us. And we're all called to light our torch and hold it high and make others in our community think about what we're saying, what we believe, what we value, because that's how we all mature and make the most of our lives. That's part of what community is, right—rubbing up against each other? Sometimes it's a smooth rub, sometimes a prickly, scratchy rub.

The Power of Authenticity

In authentic community, not only are we loved and accepted and supported, we are also lovingly challenged. Sometimes that challenge makes us think about things we have done wrong—or solidifies our thought processes. When we became mothers, God did not intend for our growth—mental, emotional, physical, spiritual—to become stunted. He meant for it to accelerate. The way we accelerate growth is to foster and nurture a seed, right? Sometimes it takes some pruning and redirecting, but nothing happens if there isn't first a seed.

Last year I bought a baby weeping willow for ten dollars. Now, my husband and I have always wanted a weeping willow, so when I saw it for such a bargain price, I was thrilled. They grow fast; in a few years it would be lovely. I searched through the five trees the nursery had, aware that they all seemed to have limbs only on one side. But I figured for ten bucks, it was worth the gamble, right? I brought one home, and my husband said, "Uh, hmm. Did you notice the branches are all on one side?" So I gave him the spiel that it was worth the ten-dollar risk and if we hated it next year, we could dig it up.

At the beginning of the summer, we noticed the baby willow was thriving. Then we left for six weeks. And when we returned, it was *really* thriving—lush with new leaves and longer branches. But it was also leaning to one side in a certain arc, all that luscious chlorophyll weighing it down. Left alone, what might look like "thriving" would ultimately kill it. (Inwardly, it seems to sense this, even sending two of its branches toward the other side, as if in a desperate grab.) So it needs me, as part of its community, to offer a small saw to take away a few of its branches over on the right, so that others will grow on the left, and balance might one day be in its future.

Let's bring this concept into the human realm. A few years ago I vividly remember sitting with my aunt, cousin, and mother at a table. I was telling them about my life, how I struggled to run a household and be a good mom and wife as well as run a company, take part in a book group, write a couple books a year, do some editing, and lead a Bible study to boot. The heart of that chat was my griping about no one else stepping forward to lead the study, so I felt that I had to do it. "They say that if you need someone to do something, ask the busiest person around. Why is that? I'm so tired of other women telling me how busy they are. Busy doing *what*? What could possibly be filling their days? If they had to do *half* of what I had to do every day, they'd be *busy*."

Blech. It pains me even to write it out and relive that moment. And to have the subject matter be Bible study, something that usually delights me . . . if you were right here beside me, you'd see me sighing heavily. My family, three women I love dearly, my community in that moment, stared back at me, eyes wide at the intensity and bitterness in my tone. I can't remember what they said. There wasn't a lot to be said in that moment. I think all three felt a bit attacked as some of *those women* I'd just complained about. There have been other times when each has said something that made me think—about my life, about how I do life. But in that moment, it was more their palpable reactions, the undercurrent that we women can tap into and feel, that made me know I had crossed the line, that I was being ugly—and sinful. Pride and bitterness had reared their heads, and I could see them both reflected in my loved ones' eyes.

I spent days thinking about what was going on in my life and how I'd landed in such a yucky place in my soul. I thought about how I needed to cut back on commitments and get a grip—that I didn't always have to be the one who came through in a pinch. I realized I was exhausted and stretched thin and this wasn't allowing me to thrive; it was encouraging the darkness within me to thrive. Like my little willow, left to continue on my warped path, I might become stunted, or worse, sick. I didn't want to be like that. I wanted to become more and more a woman who exuded love and peace and grace all the days of my life.

That is the power of authentic community—to support and encourage us but also to redirect us when we're off track and to feel accepted and supported, even when our course needs to be rerouted or when we're laying down new, straight tracks in the right direction. This encouragement is *beautiful* in the fullest sense of the word and is an act of redemption and love.

When asked, women from our survey defined "an authentic community" as people who are:

like family
caring
supportive
a fellowship
being real
able to share similar
    interests and purpose
honest and open
dependable
accepting
respectful
welcoming
vulnerable
trustworthy
their true selves
not holding up walls

committed
encouraging, even
    through failure
like iron sharpening iron
those you can laugh and
    cry with
sincere
deep, not "surface-y"
able to engage in mean-
    ingful conversation
able to share struggles
transparent
without fear of rejection
those with whom you
    feel you belong

Isn't that a lovely picture? I have found "authentic community" among my family, a few treasured friends, and yes, even in that Bible study (which I'm happily attending but *not* leading these days). I know others have found it in their neighborhood, their PTA group, playgroups (supposedly for their children but also for moms), and even online (which we'll talk about in a minute).

To be sure, this sort of community often takes years to develop, which I know is tough if, for instance, you have to move frequently. In the meantime, I hope you can rely on family or one or two dear friends to stand in the gap for you. The key, I believe, is to have common goals and find people willing to be just a bit vulnerable. If we let our walls down, we want others to do the same. And only in letting those walls down do we get to know each other on a real level and encourage growth all around.

Virtual Communities: Faux or Real?

The other day I parked my car and got out, gazing in wonder at my godchild, Eden, playing on the playground. I know it had been weeks since I had seen her, but suddenly her hair had grown at a pace equal to that of my baby weeping willow! We got closer and I realized she was wearing a hair extension. Eden, a maniacal Hannah Montana fan, was just playing a little with lovely, long locks.

I just discovered that my hairstylist, a pixielike, olive-

Do you see the value of authentic community? Do you have something that resembles this picture of authentic community? How do you think you can get closer to that ideal?

skinned beauty with long, salon-blond hair, has hair extensions—the kind that take hours to weave in and last for weeks. "My hair is thin," she said. "I have to have them."

I was shocked. After all, I had spent years envying her lovely, lush, thick hair. And it wasn't real? I was half delighted that she shared my thin-hair plight and half irritated that she had managed to fake me out.

Now really, I haven't thought of this since the day I found out, but thinking of online communities brought it to mind. Because there are literally no walls online, and people can log on with fake names. There is an uncommon freedom to "be real" or share heartfelt, deep beliefs and struggles with others. To be sure, there are echoes of "authentic community" that can happen, but there is also the capacity to pretend to be who you are not, because how would anyone know? Add to that a freedom to lash out, say things via your computer keyboard that you would never say to someone face-to-face, and often, hurt feelings are the result. Does that sound like authentic community to you?

There are places you can seek safe, closer-to-authentic communities online. You can begin your own Yahoo group and invite people you or your friends know personally. You can create a list of rules that dictate things such as respect and care and confidentiality, and "Mama Moderator" can send them out once a month to remind everyone of the playing rules. That moderator can have the power to "pull someone aside" and call her on bad behavior and even block that person from the group if said person refuses to correct her bad behavior. A moderator can also have the power to "put down the gavel" and end a conversation if it goes on too long or ceases to be beneficial to the members at large.

I've belonged to such a group since its inception several years ago. It's a group of Christian fiction writers, called ChiLibris. And now, even with more than two hundred members, it still runs incredibly smoothly because of the rules outlined above. Occasionally people do vent or get into spirited debate, but the overall intention is to serve as support and a form of community to one another. Often, after those debates, you'll see heartfelt apologies and the desire

---

Safe Internet Sites

If you're seeking safe mom forums, here are some sites of interest. (Of course, given the speed of change on the Net, half of these will probably be gone and two dozen more in their place by the time this book is published. Ask friends you trust—you'll find the good ones.)

Facebook.com—social networking, share photos/videos
MySpace.com—social networking, share photos/videos
MamaSource.com—resources and networking, in your specific community
MOPS.org—resources and social networking
CafeMom.com—social networking
Nesting.com—social networking, news, calendar, journal
Trusted author's blog—like what they said? Keep on top of what they say now. (Google their name to find them on the Net.)
Kizoodle.com—trade kid stuff, forums
Bamamoms.com—news, topics of interest for moms, forums
Meetup.com—use the Internet to get off the Internet!
Bigtent.com—safe and secure online group meeting place
Momconnection.com—*Parenting* and *BabyTalk* magazines' forums and surveys

for restoration if anyone's crossed the line. There's a serious sense of mutual respect. It's a place I can ask honest questions about the craft of writing or ask if anyone knows such things as where I can find railroad lines on a map of 1880. It's also a place where I can post a struggle about finances or questions about a deeper, theological issue I'm trying to figure out myself before I write it from my character's point of view. Except for "open mic" Saturdays, everything we post has to in some way be related to writing. But we also celebrate birthdays, send flowers (and sometimes more than flowers) to members during hard times, and join forces for group projects. Like mothering, writing can be a lonely process at times. ChiLibris makes me feel as if I'm not alone.

I know some of you have found similar outlets in chat rooms and forums on the subject of mothering or other concerns. Shannon said, "I've had really good luck with my online connections. After having a miscarriage and then being pregnant again, I found the most supportive group of women going through the same situation (pregnancy after loss). It's been over four years now and there are eight of us that still keep in touch with each other almost on a daily basis through a private blog we created. They are friends for life!" And Shawna Lee said, "I've made some long, endearing friendships on forums that have developed into more than imagined. *Years* later we keep in touch online and in real life."

I love that, and I've seen it happen too. My ChiLibris friends hold an annual retreat and many of us fly in to fellowship, learn more about the craft, share what we've learned lately, network, laugh, and pray. I think that's the litmus test of any online community: Would you want to hang out with these people for the weekend? If you can't say yes to that, it's time to look at other options—virtual or real.

Here are some other things that women mentioned about the Internet.

The Good

"I use email as a form of communication with my church and my family that live in different states."

Sherry

"I love the MOPS forums b/c they give great advice and it's encouraging. I also do Facebook some, and so far I like it b/c it connects me with friends far away."

Amy

"It is a source for me to keep in touch with friends across the country. We have moved four times in eight years and met several people who are at our stage in life and just enjoy keeping in touch. Through the Internet we get to share pictures of our families."

Anna

"I love it! It's how I gain new insight into different subjects. It's how I can stay connected to other moms, and to see how they are doing things. It gives me new and fresh ideas."

Lisa

"Email is a great way for me to communicate with many people. It allows me to write to others on my own time at all odd hours of the day/night. I don't like spending lots of time on the phone."

Sharon

"I love email, because no one can hear all the chaos in my house!"

Karen

"Many of the blogs I read encourage me as a wife, mom, and keeper of the home."

Melissa

"I like it because I grew up in a very urban area. Now I am *very* rural. So online connections keep me connected to the world."

Kirsten

"The girls in my online community are closer to me than a lot of my other friends. We move a lot, so I leave lots of groups I connect with in person; but those girls always come with me wherever we go. They also know me on a deeper level, b/c they read all of my complaining and frustrations that I don't want to burden my 'real life' friends with."

Suzie

The Bad

"Folks take stuff out of context or get feelings hurt/angry for a misunderstanding tone/wording of what was written more times than not."

Liz

"They are not real. They are nice. But no one will ever come see the real me—only the one I put on the web. I need real people in my life so I am going to be stopping the fake online stuff."

Stephanie

"I love to use the Internet to get new ideas for decorating and things to do with my kids but sometimes I spend too much time getting new ideas and not enough time actually *using* those ideas!"

Carody

"I love that there is a place where women can connect, however the anonymity can cause issues with some women. They feel that they can say whatever they want because they have a 'private' screen name and they forget that the other women have feelings."

Shawna Lee

"They can be so fake and a terrible substitute for the real thing. Communication can be skewed since body language and tone are not a part of it."

Erin

"They have their place but are not a substitute for real life relationships. Sometimes you need the actual shoulder to lean on!"

Chris

And the Ugly

"I know I spend too much time online . . . nothing inappropriate, but it takes my attention away from my family and my home. I have found online communities to be artificial and poor substitutes for genuine interaction and deepening relationships as well as quality time. I spend time online to escape stress in my life . . . to hide . . . to have something I am in control of. Guess that sounds kind of like an addiction, huh?"

Jennifer

"There are lots of drama queens and inflated egos out there."

Kris

"A negative side of the Internet is the opportunity for a 'secret life'—recently a girlfriend's niece was caught posting information on her MySpace page, which revealed she was being very deceptive to her parents. That part scares me very much."

Carole

Hey, moms! Every one of us needs an account on each of these social networks, even if it's *only* to check on our children. This is the third story within three months I've heard like this; it's part of protecting our children as they venture into this world, and training them to be accountable *everywhere*. Be aware, and tell your children you have an account on any new network that pops up, or require access to keep tabs on what they're putting on there. (I have a teen on Facebook, but I have all "friend requests" come through me, and I was her first "friend" on there.) We want them to be real and authentic too, right?

Stepping Out . . . into Community

Okay, so we've covered online communities, let's return to those we can touch and feel—our friends and extended family, our neighborhood, and our places where we meet because of a shared interest, such as a church, school, or moms' support group. This is where we reach out, dare to be vulnerable, and seek others who are looking for friendship and growth opportunities too. And as a young globa-mama, you might not be ready to tackle AIDS or finding a home for every orphan, but you can take one step closer to making the world a better place for you and your children. As Betsy said, "I'm a small impact person; I like to help those around me, dinners, errands, watching a child, or helping an elderly person." I like that. If we all did that, what would life on Planet Mom look like? Positively momutopian?

Do you have a community you trust? Why or why not? How could you find your own authentic community or grow closer to women in a current community?

As we talked about early in the chapter, one of the gifts of motherhood is often a new empathy or compassion for others. Michelle said, "I have a greater appreciation for the trying life circumstances that others go through, even though I don't necessarily know the details. I have greater patience for others' shortcomings, and I have better and more purposeful 'radar' to seek out new moms who are struggling on the inside and in need of support. I also understand and value the tremendous impact of a supportive family and church community much more than before." This is a woman *ripe* for spreading her community roots. Not only is she looking for ways to find

Healthy Online Community Guidelines/
Things to Keep in Mind

How much screen time do I want to budget myself every day?

Am I neglecting something more important by being online?

Is this encouraging me to grow as a person and therefore be a better mom?

Do I learn something, or does being online encourage me 80 percent of the time or more?

Is this a healthy group with healthy guidelines?

Is the purpose of this group one I can champion?

Does this blogger pull me forward or backward?

Do I trust most of the members' advice?

Do I leave this group feeling better or worse about myself?

Are there women on here I'd like to know in real life?

Are there women on here I'd like to become more like?

Would my pastor, mentor, and husband (or another person you respect) approve of this group's subject matter?

Is this group primarily women?

If there are men, is there a unified, rational reason to be in this group? Does conversation remain on the topic or get too personal?

Am I willing to leave this group if a man flirts with me? *(Danger! Danger! Ask yourself, What would I want my husband to do if a woman were flirting with him online?)*

Is there a moderator? Does she chime in when necessary?

Do members keep what I say confidential? Do I do the same for them?

Are there other groups I want to visit?

Before you hit "post," ask yourself, *Would I say this to her if we were face to face?*

support and love, she's also seeking ways to support and love others. It's beautiful! I can just see the community seed planted and beginning to grow and flourish!

Contrast Michelle to another respondent who said, "I've realized that raising my daughters to be the women I think God wants them to be is a harder job than I thought. I see all of the influences on them and realize that far too much is negative. And that my job is to surround them with positive influences. I've had to learn that I may be viewed as 'different' by my family, friends, church members, and the world. But as long as I'm doing what God has called me to do for *my* children, what other people think shouldn't affect me."

Hey, I'm all for standing for what you believe, particularly if you have clear direction from the Big Man (and even more if you can point to scriptural support). But boy, this mama sounds *lonely*! I want to help her find friends, authentic community! Surely, there is one other woman within sixty miles who thinks the way she does and will love her as a sister would.

And if not, maybe she needs to rethink her stance. It concerns me that everyone dear to her, along with her standing communities, all sound like they disagree with her methods. Granted, I'm visualizing a remote ranch and the possibility of a man with seven wives, but really, we have to be willing to ask ourselves at all times: *Am I on the right track? Is this best for my family and me long term? How does this compare to others and what they believe? Can I find others who think like me?* If not, we're disassociating from our potential communities within our extended family, neighborhood, or shared interest group.

Remember, walls are supposed to be coming down not going up.

Social Activist Mama . . . or Not

There are moments in every mother's life when she gapes at the evening news, wondering how people could be so evil to one another. We ask ourselves: *Why are people so mean and cruel? How can they continue to survive, with that going on? What if that were happening here, on my street? What will all of this look like when my baby is grown?* There are three ways to go when faced with bigger-than-I-am-questions: the fear route, the bury-my-head-in-the-sand route, or the crusader route.

Along the fear route, we get overwhelmed by it all—AIDS, war, terrorism, genocide, pollution, the falling value of the U.S. dollar. Closer to home it may be a child molester reportedly trolling in our neighborhood (or living around the corner), poor quality of water, or gangs tagging our walls. The fear route often turns into the bury-my-head-in-the-sand route, because we can't summon the mental energy to process all that need, let alone the emotional energy our fear churns up. Some opt to move straight to bury-my-head, refusing even to watch the news or read a paper or receive information on the Internet, hoping if they don't know, it will somehow not hurt them or those they love. But part of raising children to be healthy adults is teaching them how to deal with reality and cope with fear, so we need to figure out how to do those things first.

How can you deal with reality? Become informed. Receive the news in some format you can digest easily and routinely. Find sources you trust, but then salt them with the opposition's voice here and there—it makes us all think for ourselves, not just accept the party line. For instance, I write children's books that feature polar bears. For years, I've heard of the plight of polar bears because global warming is eating up their icy home. This has alarmed me, moved me. But yesterday I heard the governor of Alaska say that the polar bear population has never been more healthy—and they are more than three hundred thousand strong. Hmm . . . so now I have to do a little more research and find out the truth. It illustrates the fact that all news seems to have a subjective spin to it these days; we need to invest enough into our world knowledge in order to come to our own conclusions.

Personally I like to read *Time* magazine and watch the NBC evening news. You might be more of a *U.S. News & World Report* and Fox News girl. You might like to read the local paper each day or you might simply prefer to subscribe to several blogs and get it all via the Internet. Some weeks I just don't have time or energy to read more than the first paragraph of each article in *Time*. But there are more restful, easier weeks when I can read the whole thing, cover to cover. Sometimes I rip out an article to read later, when I have more mental energy. And sometimes my magazines stack up for months. The point is, I *try* to stay informed. And then, when my children ask me about why the bad men flew planes into the buildings on 9/11, I have the information I need to discuss it with them.

How do you stay informed on news and current events in your community and the world? Is that enough?

This also helps me get a grip on world issues so I can see how I might help, in some small way here or there, become a "mini crusader" for what I believe. I think the greatest way to build bridges with others is to reach out in ways that touch their lives—mosquito nets for children in Malawi, sponsoring a child through Compassion International or World Vision in war-torn nations, writing your congressman, packing a Christmas box for Operation Christmas Child. If you open your mind and pay attention to the many ways we're called to help others, they present themselves. It doesn't have to be huge. It can be one small thing a year and then three small things a year, and see where it goes from there.

Facts and *action* are my two main ways to deal with fear. If I can learn all the facts—not hype but facts—I'm able to see a situation more reasonably. If there are gangs moving into my neighborhood, the fear part of my brain says, *We have to move! We're in desperate danger! I don't want my kids going to school with gang members!* (The bury-my-head part would say, *They painted on my wall? What wall? I don't see any wall.*) But if I calmly look at the facts, even call my local police station and chat with an officer about my concern, I might find out that there is a gang nearby, but it's really just five teen boys who are trying to prove something and that the police have their eye on them. He might tell me there are five bad boys but encourage me to remember that there are six hundred *good* boys at the local high school. Whew. Balance is always a good thing.

> What scares you about your community or the greater world? What small step could you take to fight against that fear and help right what you see is wrong?

And if I took *action* by calling my local neighborhood watch, adding a sign for my street; if I called all my neighbors and told them to turn on their porch lights when these guys walk by, then I would not feel powerless. I would feel powerful. In some small way I would be making my children's world a better, safer place. (And in turn I might even encourage those five bad boys to bail on the gang thing because they're not faking anyone out anyway.)

Maybe we need to convince our school to take on pen pals in the Middle East or our church to support a missionary deep in Muslim territory or maybe we could do something even closer to home, even smaller. Maybe we could reach out to our new neighbor, take part in a random acts of kindness day, or pick up the phone and call an elderly acquaintance just to say she's on our mind and we'd like to drop by with some extra cookies we just made. There are millions of opportunities to make this great world a better place.

So how else can we take action before fear gets its iron grip on us? We asked survey respondents "How has becoming a mom made you want to impact your neighborhood, school, church, city, or the world? How do you act on these desires?" And they said:

join online communities with social issues focus

support charities

volunteer

reach out to others by phone, mail, or visits

strive to impact one person at a time within my sphere of influence

advocate for a cause

pray

make meals for others

donate money
be friendly
be kind
watch for ways to help in the moment
reach out to the lonely
make my home a haven for others
school involvement
smile
kind words
take part in my children's causes
host neighborhood gatherings
Meals on Wheels
short-term missions trips

be a listener versus a helper
work through professional associations
join committees
write letters to the editor
circulate petitions
volunteer at church
adopt Compassion International children with birthdays the same as my kids'
be involved at a nursing home
open my home to neighborhood kids

Great ideas, all. But still, more often than not, we don't act. We asked why, and here's what people said:

fatigue
can't see what I can change
overwhelmed
fear of being judged
young children
time constraints
lack of planning
no direction

laziness
selfishness
insecurity
feeling unqualified
"little me, big world"
lack of money
fear of overstepping boundaries
distraction

| need for childcare | lack of spousal support |
| not knowing where to begin | fear of rejection |

Just like anything else, if it's important to us, we risk and we expend the energy. And sometimes we have to table world crusader desires for the home crusader desires for a season. Sonia said, "Every time I try to start something, whether it be at church or in my neighborhood, one of the girls gets sick or there is some other thing that comes up. I couldn't understand for the longest time why this was happening. And I then began to seek the Lord about it and felt him telling me that it's not my season right now, that I am trying to build my dreams; I'm trying to make them happen on my own accord. God really wants me to be still and learn from this season that I am in with my children and being a stay-at-home mom. The Scripture that I felt impressed in my heart was 'Unless the Lord builds the house, the laborers build in vain.'"

Amen to that, sister. Maybe this is your season for rest and concentration on your children. I get that—I really do. But if you are alarmed or fearful, don't let those negative emotions churn within you; it will waste precious and limited energy. Combat fear with facts, balance, and action in equal measure and I believe you'll stay on top of it, giving your children the sense of peace and security they need.

And if you're sitting this season out, support those who will make a difference out there. Rauscha said, "As a mom, you see a lot of negative things, but also more positive things going on. There are a lot of people really trying to help make things better out there." Heroes, they're called, waging war against the darkness, giving us hope in the light. Because even though we globa-mamas might occasionally get lost and overwhelmed with what's happening out in the world, we know firsthand that there is always hope, always goodness, always love. We just have to reach out and grab the nearest living examples and give them a big hug and smooch.

Mamas of the Round Table Discussion Questions

1. Do you currently have "authentic community"? Why or why not?
2. Do you take part in online communities—blogs, forums, chat rooms? What good things do you gain from them?
3. How much does your immediate or extended family support you? Do you enjoy spending time with them? If you weren't related, would you still do so?
4. How have you reached out to others in your neighborhood or meeting place (school, church, playgroup, or other) to bond in a vulnerable, real way? Can you see other ways to do so?
5. Would you describe yourself as fearful, bury-my-head, or crusader mom, or none of the above? Why or why not?
6. Share three things you love about this period of time for our nation and our world and the opportunities for you and your family therein.

6

A Father's
Love

how becoming a mom changes
your relationship with God

My relationship with God was waning before I had children. Then I knew I wanted my girls to develop a relationship with Christ, so I began attending church again—for the girls. God has since reminded me that what is most important is for me to focus on my relationship with him.

Natalie

The deep, overwhelming love I have for my children has opened my eyes to the kind of deep, deep love that God has for his children.

Sharon

I wish I had more time for God. At this stage of life, he gets short prayers and conversations instead of lengthy quiet times. And my Bible reading is often restricted to the kids' Bible!

Ali

Ten days after the marathon, Jen lay in a quiet hospital room, utterly aware of the silence and warmth—the heady presence of God. Her friends had come and gone. Alex had taken Nina home for the night, and it was just her with her precious new little baby girl, Adelaine. She knew she could put the perfectly wrapped bundle in her bassinet, right beside the bed, but right now she couldn't get enough of her. Couldn't get over the fact that her baby was here at last, two weeks after her due date, two weeks after she finally understood she was going to be the mother of two . . . and she was happy about it.

She was thankful for these last fourteen days, uncomfortable as they had been. She'd been sleeping in the recliner downstairs, suffering from too much acid reflux to be prone beside her husband, not that she had been sleeping at all. Instead she'd paced the floor, willing her body to begin labor, her mind spinning. She spent the time talking to God, confessing her sorrow over her reticence to acknowledge this new change in life, her slow acceptance of the gift a baby always is. All she could figure out was that she was overwhelmed at the idea of change.

But now, holding this baby, Jen couldn't imagine not having her. Slow tears crested her lids and slid down her cheeks. She lifted the bundle—impossibly light, had Nina ever been this light?—and gently kissed the baby's cheeks. Adelaine squirmed as if her mother were disturbing her, and Jen laughed under her breath. She cradled the babe in her arms and stared down at the perfection, ignoring the stork bite on her forehead that would fade in time. "You are good to me, beyond good," she said to God in a whisper. "Thank you for this child's safe arrival. Thank you for being with us. Thank you for blessing us. Thank you for opening up my heart to this new little one, Father. I am . . . amazed."

And it was then that she heard it, a few notes, in her mind. The music that had been silent edged closer and then faded, like a wave on the sand—just a few notes, over and over again.

A night nurse came in. "Want me to take that baby to the nursery so you can grab a little sleep?"

"That might be good. I'm very tired. But right now, I have a sudden urge to play the piano."

The nurse slowly blinked in her direction. "Excuse me?"

"A piano. Is there one in the hospital?"

"One in the foyer, but there's no way they'll let you play it at this hour." She filled Jen's water bottle and placed it on her tray. "There is another. In the chapel, one floor up."

"The chapel? Can I go there now? Play, if I do it quietly?"

"Not without me to walk you up. No patient of mine is going to give birth and then go traipsing around in the middle of the night. My shift is just about over. You mind a little company? Or must this be a solo tour?"

Jen laughed a little. "No, you can come." Usually she froze up when others were around, listening to her play. But right now, the song was emerging in her head, the notes diving and soaring in her mind. She lifted Adelaine up in her hands and kissed her cheeks. "It's you!" she whispered. "My little muse!"

The nurse left and then soon returned with a wheelchair and she insisted Jen ride in it. Jen decided to keep her baby with her, and the nurse agreed to hold her as she played. They moved up the elevator and out into a quiet hall of what looked like offices, past the cafeteria, gated shut and dark, and down to the end of a hall, where there was a small, elegant chapel.

Soft light illuminated an undulating wave, which emanated from a carved dove, behind a bold, high-armed cross. To the right was a grand piano.

On shaking legs, Jen rose and faced the cross. "Thank you, Lord," she whispered, "for this child's safe delivery. Thank you for awakening love in my heart for her. And this music . . . I've missed the music, God."

The nurse took the babe from her arms and sat down in the front row, in deep shadow. A stream of light cascaded down on the piano bench, and as Jen sat down, the song burst wide and full within her mind, and she began to play without hesitation.

A Sacrificial Love

Say we were dear friends, on a girls' getaway to London (hey, a girl can dream, right?). We're walking along, and you step into the street, commenting on how cute that red phone booth is up there, blissfully unaware that a double-decker bus is hurtling toward you.

Since we're dear friends, I hope that I would burst into action and push you out of the way, even if it meant that I might die.

I hope. Because I love my friends.

But I don't know.

Deep down, I can visualize myself screaming, "Look out!" I can almost feel the horror at what I am watching, terror sending adrenaline rushing through my body, but would that cause me to save you and sacrifice myself? Uh, maybe. My friends are important to me. There are a few I consider so close that I can't imagine living without them. But I'm worried that in that critical moment, I would choose self-preservation over self-sacrifice. (If we ever cross paths in real life, you can decide for yourself whether you can trust me to be your pal!)

But as a mom, I *know* I would do anything possible to save my children. I want to see them live to adulthood, become all they were created to be. I know you feel the same way. And while few of us will have to make such a dramatic sacrifice for our children, we all sacrifice in small ways every day to help them grow and flourish. We sacrifice sleep, the TV show we'd rather watch, and gourmet coffee for the economy brand, energy to shop for and make healthy food, down time on the computer so he can log on to Nic Jr., and doing ten loads of laundry. The list goes on and on. But we do it with pleasure because we love our children. We want to provide for them and surround them with love and protection and good things.

This is a lot like God. Now, I've been a Christian all my life and felt as though I've had a pretty good relationship with him. But becoming a mom escalated things. Finally I have fully grasped what unconditional love means, as I have felt such love for my children. Survey responses echo something similar:

"I have a deeper understanding of how God views me. I love my daughter so much and I am so proud and honored to be her mom. It helps me understand how God views me."

Marissa

"I think about how much I love my child and know that God loves me a million times more than that."

Jean

"It is easier to picture God as a father and understand how much he loves me. If I care about *my* children this much, then I can't even imagine how dear I am to him!"

Bethany

"He loves us *no matter what*. His love is intense and personal."

Elizabeth

It got more specific for me too, like Elizabeth's "intense and personal" comment. Suddenly the dark days of remembrance leading up to Easter moved me to tears. I could see Jesus hanging on the cross, feel the deep, pulsing grief of watching someone I love be put to death; but it was thinking of his mother Mary, kneeling at his bloody feet, weeping—it makes me cry even now. And for God to sacrifice his Son, for him to put Mary through such agony, *so that I might be free, so that I might never be separated from him*, is something the significance of which motherhood has only magnified.

He loves me so much that he put his Son, part of himself, in front of a double-decker bus for me, without hesitation—knowing he would die, so that I might live.

He loves you that much too.

A Cozy, Close Relationship

Now, some of my non-mom friends clearly get this *without* motherhood. I'm just a little more dense. But here's the second big thing, after sacrificial love, that motherhood taught me about my God. He also wants intimacy with each of us—a *real* relationship, just as we crave a relationship with our child.

John Eldredge writes in *Walking with God*:

> It is our deepest need, as human beings, to learn to live intimately with God. It is what we were made for. Back in the beginning of our story, before the fall of man, before we sent the world spinning off its axis, there was a paradise called Eden. In that garden of life as it was meant to be, there lived the first man and woman. Their story is important to us because whatever it was they were, and whatever it was they had, we also were meant to be and to have. And what they enjoyed above all the other delights of that place was this—they walked with God. They talked with him, and he with them. For this you and I were made. And this we *must* recover.[9]

I adore how Eldredge sees things and puts them into perspective. Here he's placed us in "that old Adam and Eve story," and made us see how God sees all of *us* as his children, just as he viewed Adam and Eve. In that first story of people in Genesis, we discover that people abode with their God literally in a physical way. And it doesn't stop there. Throughout the Bible we see God drawing near,

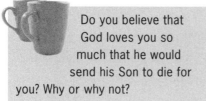

Do you believe that God loves you so much that he would send his Son to die for you? Why or why not?

calling out, urging his people to move. And his people respond. Or they don't.

He's not just a parental or father figure to us, he's also the lover of our souls, tenderly whispering to us, curving an arm around our backs, hoping we will nestle in. This might be a new concept to you or maybe one you haven't revisited for a while. The beautiful thing about parenthood is that we have all these new opportunities to think through things again, don't we? Or think through them for the first time. More than 80 percent of our survey respondents reported a significant change in their relationship with God after becoming a mom. Here are some comments about understanding and perception:

"I remember the first Christmas after I became a mom. The Christmas story and the birth of Jesus hit me in a whole new way, even though I had been a Christian for most of my life. The meaning of Easter deepened for me too. I remember thinking that there are a few people in this world that I would be willing to die for. But I can tell you there is *no one* that I would give my son for. My understanding of God's unfathomable love is definitely deeper now than before I became a mom."

Vickie

"It took a little time, but I learned that God is not big and scary and out to get me. No God who gave me these two children could be. I learned to think of him as the parent I want to be."

Sasha

"Before trying to get pregnant and having miscarriages and then having my children and having developmental issues with them, I had never experienced real tragedy in my life. My faith had not been put to the test. After

159

going through many trials, I can stand firm and rest in complete peace with knowing that God is sovereign and always faithful."

Jennifer

"I am trying to get a better grasp of how God loves me as I learn about loving my children. I have never really felt totally confident in God's love and grace—it always seemed performance-driven. So I am really trying to change my ideas as I learn how to love my kids and use that to see how God sees me as his child."

Carla

Love Unearned

I think we all have wrestled or will wrestle with the performance-based idea about God's love. But just as we love our children, no matter what they do, God's love for us will never cease. And his grace—purchased at such a steep and unfathomable price as Christ's death—is nothing we can ever earn. You and I can't feed enough starving children; we cannot build enough houses for the poor; we cannot teach enough Sunday school; we cannot cook enough for our ailing neighbor; we cannot write or read enough Christian books—whatever it is we think we can do to *earn* his grace, it is *not enough*. Period.

It is a lot like how I love each of my children. I look at each of them and think, *Man, I love that kid*. Do they do things that irritate me? Yes. Have they hurt, frustrated, and angered me? Yes. But the bigger picture is love—enjoyment, connection, relationship. *I love these children*, I think, staring at each of them, peacefully sleeping in their beds after a long day, more than I could have imagined.

And that's how God looks at us. Even when we fail him and fail each other, he loves us. We are enough, solely because *Christ* is enough. He stands in the gap, cleanses our sins as if he were an EMT on the battlefield, cleaning out the infection and filling it with salve that will make us whole. Because God loves us that much.

So not only are we totally forgiven, we are *desired*, *pursued*, *longed for*. Accepting Christ as our Savior, accepting God's call to peace, acceptance, love, and care, is the greatest gift we can give him. He celebrates as each one of us comes to understand these great truths. After all, we were created for relationship with him—to love and worship him freely and to know his presence in our lives. When we discover what that means (and it's a lifelong process of discovery), we edge closer and closer to him.

I've been in email communication with a reader who has an eighteen-year-old son whom she loves very much, but who has left home. "I guess you can't call it running away

---

The Lowdown on Sin, Forgiveness, and Grace

Don't have a Bible handy? Log on to www.BibleGateway.com and pop in these verses to read them for yourself.

Romans 10:9–10	1 Corinthians 6:11
Acts 16:31	Ephesians 2:8–10
1 John 3:2	Titus 3:3-7
1 John 3:24	

from home, when they're eighteen," she said. "He's left home. The only thing we hear are horror stories he tells his grandmother. He refuses to speak to us."

One of my mother's friends just died, and her son has been on the streets for years, in and out of drugs. When she knew she was dying, she was asked if they should find her son and tell him that his mother would soon be gone; she refused.

I shake my head and wonder over the grace and strength it takes to parent the prodigal. *Please not me*, I say to God, thinking of my own children, glad they're still at an age when Mom rules. But at some point it will be up to them. How much they talk to me, think of me, hear me, seek me out will depend on them. They'll be grown-ups, and I'll still be hungering for relationship with them, but will they want the same from me? Will they want to know me in a mature relationship? Will our relationship be ever deepening, intimate, bonded? Or will we drift apart?

This is how it is with us and God. He's spoon-fed us, babied us, and gently called to us—through friends, things we've read, things we've heard; sometimes through our children. Some of us might be recognizing this for the first time, now, as adults, this understanding that God wants something more from us, something living, interesting, vital, primary—*a connection*. Some of us may have

> "When I became a mom, I realized how much I need God in my life. I could not get through a day without him giving me patience, energy, and peace of mind! He gave me these precious boys to take care of and I feel so blessed to have the opportunity to help them know him better as they grow."
>
> *Jackie*

walked the prodigal's walk for a time, turning away from Love. Some of us have always been in some sort of relationship with the Big Guy but we've let him get only so close. Regardless of where we've been, there is always something more, something deeper to discover. We cannot out-experience God. We cannot know him fully, this side of heaven. But we can get an awful lot closer.

> Have you experienced any sort of intimate relationship with God? How might you take a step forward in becoming closer to him?

He wants to. And deep down, I think we all do too.

The Papa Road

Robin Gunn was the first one to talk to me about how she refers to God as "Daddy" or "Papa," drawing on the biblical name of Abba (not the seventies music group sort of Abba; rather, the Alpha and the Omega—the beginning and the end sort of Abba). Her intimate terms startled me, shook me, but gradually I adopted them too, tried them out in conversation with my God, because I could sense what she knew already—that he was invitational, warm, welcoming.

Once we settle into life with God, we begin to sense him more and more, particularly in how he guides us, leads us. All along God is trying to help us lead the best, fullest, finest lives possible. When we know him intimately, we realize that he tries to warn us of bad paths and leads us onto better ones. When a woman is pocketing petty cash from the office drawer, even though she thinks she has justification, I think she literally has to shake off Papa's hand of warning, of conviction. Or the woman who thinks her husband doesn't see her anymore and pretends to be single online "just to escape," but is really aiming to attract attention, if she has an intimate relationship with God, I think God would be calling to her, asking her to come near him, seek him for what she's missing and longing for—love. That's how he deals with me. Over and over I sense him taking my hand like a loving, earthly father might, and whispering, "Come. This way. It's the right way."

Sometimes I'm the stubborn two-year-old, stomping my feet and turning the other way, just to be defiant. But it always comes down better if I welcome his touch, his call, his guidance. If I take his hand and follow where he leads me, that's when life is best. Natalie said, "Since I've become a mom, God feels much more present, and I seek his example and instruction more for my role as a mother and for my marriage."

Natalie has it down. If we could fill our minds with his Word, seeking his instruction and his Spirit for guidance on day-to-day things and his Son to heal us of the wounds that keep us from him and the Father to hold us when we ache, and continually praise him for all the fine gifts he has given us—children, family, friends, a job, flowers on the hillside, food on the table, whatever!—suddenly, we are in full-on, joyful relationship with our Maker. Living, vital, breathing relationship. And the more we "get" that relationship, the more we invest, the less his enemy can take up our time and energy. He can cover and protect us from evil, but we must choose him over all else.

A Love without Limits

But does he care about how you're so weary of washing a preschooler's sheets, trying to toilet train him through the night, that you could scream? Yes! He can sustain you, give you strength. Does he care about how you're going crazy, after hearing yet another *Dora* or *Sponge Bob* rerun? Yes! He can give you patience and lead you to other reading material or even a TV episode that will use your adult brain. Does he care about the fact you are getting a little bored with your husband? Yes! He can rejuvenate your passion and help you remember why you fell in love with that man in the first place.

Just as you love and care for every part of your child's life—mental, emotional, physical, spiritual—so does God love and care for you. Just as you long to hear, smell, touch, and feel your child, so does God long for you. Just as you hope to teach your children about how to live a rich and fulfilling life, so does God wish to teach you. And just as you hope to train your children not to do bad things or make bad choices, so does God wish to train you too.

Love Defined

You've probably read the following Bible passage or heard it at a wedding. I love the poetic nature of my Bible's version, but here it is from *The Message* to help you read it, really read it, rather than read *over* it. Consider beginning with this prayer:

> "Open my eyes, Lord. Let me understand you in a new way. Let me know love, really know love, and reflect your love to those around me. Amen."

To understand and embody Love better than ever will only improve every relationship you have.

The Way of Love

If I speak with human eloquence and angelic ecstasy but don't love, I'm nothing but the creaking of a rusty gate.

If I speak God's Word with power, revealing all his mysteries and making everything plain as day, and if I have faith that says to a mountain, "Jump," and it jumps, but I don't love, I'm nothing.

If I give everything I own to the poor and even go to the stake to be burned as a martyr, but I don't love, I've gotten nowhere. So, no matter what I say, what I believe, and what I do, I'm bankrupt without love.

> Love never gives up.
> Love cares more for others than for self.
> Love doesn't want what it doesn't have.
> Love doesn't strut,
> Doesn't have a swelled head,
> Doesn't force itself on others,
> Isn't always "me first,"
> Doesn't fly off the handle,
> Doesn't keep score of the sins of others,
> Doesn't revel when others grovel,
> Takes pleasure in the flowering of truth,
> Puts up with anything,
> Trusts God always,
> Always looks for the best,
> Never looks back,
> But keeps going to the end.

1 Corinthians 13:1–7 *Message*

The Long Arm of the Lord: Discipline

After *love,* women from the survey mentioned *discipline* as the main "aha" they've had about God since becoming a mother. Now, I believe that God can act in a physical way. Right now I'm supposed to get this chapter written but I'm giving in to distraction, despite my passion for the subject, and I keep trying to log on to my email or Facebook, which is normally easy to do but today won't seem to work. If you could see me, you'd watch me sigh heavily and roll my eyes at God and mutter, "Okay! All right! I know this is more important!" and return to it, just as if I were a delinquent teen trying to sneak out of the house when I knew very well that I had chores to do before I went anywhere.

Some might question if God would work that way, but I don't. He knows I'm stubborn, and I need his help to keep me on track. I asked him to keep me on track today. And I believe if he can create the world, knit together my children in the womb, it's not beyond his capacity to put a crimp in my Outlook or Google links. (But please, Lord, let it only be temporarily down!)

Over the years he's had to discipline me in far more painful ways, trying to get my attention. He's let me wander far—far enough to be bartending on Sundays—and then called me home, back to his side, tail tucked between my legs. He's let me build up hopes in myself and my capabilities, sure that I was handing a publisher the Next Big Thing, then reminded me that he is supposed to be the Only Big Thing in my life and that he will personally provide for my family. (That book did diddly-squat in sales—a book I'd worked on for a *year*. But the book he woke me up in the middle of the night to write and took me just three hours? It's outsold my other twenty-nine books *combined*.) He convicts me when I open my big mouth and spew negative or sarcastic or unkind things, as clearly as if he'd just washed my mouth out with soap. He wakes me up early on Sunday mornings when I've decided to skip church and sleep in, reminding me that he's still God, whether I'm honoring him in church or not. (*All right, all right, already!* I groan, then usually get ready and go to worship.)

So this whole discipline thing never ends for us. We get a decent crack at our children from age zero to eighteen, but he's ever about refining us, teaching us, molding us closer to his image, throughout our lives. And the more malleable, flexible, willing we are to accept his discipline, the easier it goes down. (Think of it from a parent's perspective. Is it less traumatic to discipline a stubborn, willful child or an open, ready child?) And the more he sculpts us, the more we're shaped to echo all the goodness and joy in him. We were created in his image, after all.

Here are some other ways survey respondents saw God illuminated through the discipline issue:

"It only takes a trial of watching your children struggle through a situation to understand how God can be pained when we choose to make decisions that are contrary to his Word. The way I continue to love my children even when they make mistakes or when I grow angry with them gives me just a glimpse of how I imagine God must feel about us. Having the mother-child relationship also illustrates how God gives us the rules to live by but also gives us the free will to follow and believe those rules. What an awesome responsibility it is to care for each one of us the way that God does!"

Kelly

"I can more clearly see God at work in my life and the lives of others around me. I can also see how difficult it must be for God to watch us fail or struggle throughout our lives. (It's tough to watch your child struggling and not be able to do anything but stay quietly by her side so that you can be there for her when she falls or asks for help.)"

Michelle

The Problem of Pain

Some from the survey mentioned pain and tragedy and how these experiences have distanced them from God. Jill said, "I suffered three pre-term losses, two at eleven weeks and one at twenty weeks, and that certainly caused a change in my relationship with God. Things have never been the same. I don't necessarily blame God for what happened but I don't understand it either."

I do not know why God saves, heals, or blesses at times and other times does not. But I do believe that God has his eye not only on your present and future but also your child's and your future grandchild's. Not only that, but he has his eye on the path of each of *those* that each of *you* (and your progeny) will touch, interact with, love. His ultimate goal is for us to acknowledge him as God, God, God, and compel others to do the same. The way he achieves that goal is often far more complex than we can ever imagine. So because I believe that God is always faithful and always loving and always with us, I believe that he is trustworthy. I choose to put my hand in his and move forward with him, even when I don't understand.

Don't we ask the same of our children? Don't we show them how we love and care for them by our constant attention every day? Don't we hope that they trust us, even when they don't understand? Consider a child who wants to climb a cliff face, but his mother tells him no. He sees adventure, glory. She sees potential danger. Or the older child who desires a friendship, but his parents see a troubled, angry child in that friend who might lead their son astray.

Faithful + Loving + Present = Trustworthy

But those are easy examples, right? Our family experienced excruciating pain, firsthand, when our only niece, just six years old, died one night. She hugged her parents, said her last "love you," and breathed her last breath in the darkest watches of the night. She was a hard-won, treasured child, born to faithful parents. *Why, why, why?* I railed at God, angry, betrayed, bewildered. *Why not save that child, an only child? Why not intervene and heal her heart? Why not alert the doctor that there was a dangerous defect?* There were no answers to my questions. I knew that God was capable; I'd seen others healed, but here, *here*, he had chosen not to act. Nothing rational made sense. I couldn't figure out how God could use such horror and sorrow for anything good at all.

You may have experienced the same thing, or maybe your "death" was the death of a marriage, a friendship, a dream. I can't answer the why question. Becoming a mom doesn't give you the insider answer on all of life's mysteries. But I can choose to answer my God when he whispers, "Trust me. You are not alone through this. I know it hurts. I feel your pain. I am sorry it is yours to endure. But you are not bearing it alone. I share it. I have known pain, greater than this, even. And if you allow it, even this pain, this awful, gnawing, gaping wound in your heart can bring you closer to me."

God doesn't like death. God is life. He meant us to live forever, here on earth, but long ago that dream was revised. And in a fallen world, bad, bad things happen. But Good is present and has made a way for us to live forever, with him in heaven.

He can manage our questions and accusations like a loving parent. He can endure our railing at him, our beating against his chest; he can hold us close until our fury wanes and we sink, in weariness and defeat, into his arms. At that point he carries us and soothes us and bit by bit begins to heal us. But we have to allow it. And we have to accept that he uses all things, *all things*, for his good purposes. And our lives, as all-encompassing and absorbing as they are, are but a few short blips on the vast EKG of God's timeline.

We still miss Mady. Her parents still "walk with a limp" as a pastor said to me once, largely healed, but scarred forever by their loss and striving to redefine their lives. We have attempted to redeem part of this time as we've mourned. I believe as a family we have become more empathetic to those who are hurting, more willing to lean on our God. We have come to a place of peace, knowing that we cannot figure everything about God out. Part of him will forever be a mystery. We have invested more energy into learning what we can about heaven. We've learned the importance of honoring a person's memory and anticipate with excitement seeing Mady again. But would I trade it all to have that precious little girl back? Without a question.

God, God, God. Not me. God.

I choose to trust you, Father, over and over again, because you are good and mighty and faithful and my Savior, Jesus. Even when I don't understand, I will stand where you place me. I will love you and worship you as all that I am not. God, God, God, teach me, mold me, make me more like you. Amen.

A Little Child Will Lead Them

God does indeed use everything and everyone he can to reach out to us. A word from a trusted friend, something someone says on the radio that sticks with us all day, an act of kindness from a stranger, all smell like God to me. But he also speaks clearly to us through our children, making us think, making us decide what we really believe.

I have a friend who was raised as a "cultural Christian," something her family did but never really invested their hearts in. Now she and her husband don't attend church and haven't really decided what they think about Christ. When her firstborn was three years old, she said, "You can't believe all the questions this kid is asking about God. 'Where does he live? How do you know he loves us? Why don't we go to church?' "

I just smiled and inhaled a great big whiff of my God in action.

This weekend I was at a party and met a lovely British couple. We conversed for a long time, connecting on various subjects. At some

Have you ever experienced pain and grief? If so, did it drive you closer to God or further away from him? Why?

point they mentioned they'd sent their daughter to a Christian school, and she often begged them to go to church. "Oh," I said, "do you guys have a home church?"

"No," the mom said. "To tell you the truth, we've had some run-ins with some rather awful people who professed to be Christians. One was a pervert, really. It turned us off to the whole deal."

"I can understand that," I said. "It's terrible when you run into people like that. We're not perfect either, but we're pretty real and easy to get to know. And you'd like our pastor—he's a take-me-or-leave-me kind of guy—not a lot of pretense or pressure. Maybe sometime you can come and try our church."

They nodded and smiled, probably just blowing me off, but we departed on warm enough terms and I'd like to see them again. And maybe God will use that conversation, on top of their daughter's urging, to get them to try out life in fellowship. This faith thing is *so* much easier when you have a church family surrounding you.

A few other moms mentioned how God was using their children to shape their faith:

> "The blessing of our son has changed my view on God. Our son makes you think in very theological ways and had made my husband and me delve into some deep thinking and prayer and reading on subjects that we never would have, if he wasn't here to ask his questions."
>
> Megan

> "I had a lot of doubts and questions growing up and even when I got married. But that all seemed to change after my kids started asking a lot about God and it changed even more

Can you see one way God might be reaching out to you through your children? How so? Was it something they did or said, or something they do or say every day?

when my children started attending a Christian preschool. They had chapel time and it really sparked their interest. We have since been going to church on a regular basis and the kids love it. My son pays attention and really loves the music. I still have a few questions and doubts that I am working through, but I feel closer than I have ever felt before."

Rauscha

"My kids have a childlike faith that God reminds me I need to have. I see God more compassionate and loving."

Kathy

God will use whatever method he can to reach across the chasm and make us recognize his love. And children are a natural vehicle because they accept him as we were taught to, "as little children." What does that mean, to come as little children? Think of your son or daughter drawing near you, wanting nothing but time and attention, faithful, loyal, eager to learn, desiring connection and relationship, freely giving and receiving love.

Yes, if we could just bottle a bit of that up every day, we could get so much closer to him. It wouldn't just be him moving closer to us. It would be us sidling up to him. God has given us children, not only to care for and nurture but also to model his love for us. And once we recognize it, our relationship with him is forever changed and enhanced—a double blessing! We have a relationship with a child to call *our* own and another with a God who calls us *his* own.

Mamas of the Round Table Discussion Questions

1. Would you throw yourself in front of a bus—sacrifice yourself—to save your friend? How about your child? How do you know?
2. What is it about sacrifice that depicts a whole other dimension of love?
3. Do you believe that God wants an intimate relationship with you? How have you sensed that or experienced that in your life? Or how do you hope to?
4. Has God disciplined you at some point to teach you something? When, where, and how?
5. Have you experienced a hurt or tragedy that made you doubt God? Have you been able to get past your doubt? If so, how?
6. What has your child done or said that made you think about God more? Do you believe he really uses people to speak to you, reach you, on his behalf? Why or why not?

Conclusion

A Final Word . . . I Know, I Know, Enough Already!

Well, thanks for spending some of your valuable time with me and your sisters from the survey. Hopefully, you've found some comfort and inspiration and insight. I know how lonely your road might feel at times—as if you truly have been abandoned on an alien planet—or perhaps you're with a lot of people, but they all appear slightly different, as if they've been taken over by aliens! Trust that the God who made you, the God who made them, will show you the way to make the most of each relationship and look for how he's directing you, urging you. Often I find that God "whispers" by a tug on my heart, an impulse that seems right, an urge to move. See if that's how he "speaks" to you too.

As I wrapped up chapter 6, I realized that three things emerged in each chapter; whether we're discussing ourselves or our relationship with a spouse, friend, family, community, or our relationship with God, all demand time, attention, and mental/emotional investment. That's the dirty rotten truth about relationships—they take some effort. Sorry, no shortcuts to offer. So right about now, you're probably pulling out your hair, gritting your teeth, and saying, "Lisa, just where do you think I'm going to find time, attention, and mental/emotional investment?"

Whoa, whoa, don't freak. It's going to be okay, I promise. Remember, we're women. Relationships are the most important thing in our lives. I realize that when children are small and constantly in need of you, it is difficult. That's what the whole "season" thing is about.

The "Barely Surviving It" Season

Even if you're in the "barely surviving it" season, you can touch on each of your most important relationships every day. Ignored relationships can become wounded relationships, which in the long run will take your energy to heal. So what if you spent five minutes, just five minutes, of each day taking care of the big six: God, self, spouse, extended family, friends, community/world? I'm talking thirty minutes to take basic care of your most important relationships. Do it when the kids are napping, before they wake in the morning, or right after they go to bed at night. You can set a timer, if you want, to keep yourself on track. And if you're a career mom, you could even do this every day during your lunch hour. What might those thirty minutes look like? Here are some examples:

God: Find a daily devotional to read—in book form or online. Then in five minutes of quiet, read it.

Self: Heat up one of those neck pillows you throw in the microwave and sit, still and quiet, thinking about your life. Count each of your blessings, even if it's the same blessings you counted yesterday. Think about the devotional you just read, and how it applies to your life. Say a prayer.

Spouse: Email your husband at work or draft an email to send him later, telling him that he's one of your blessings. Thank him for something specific he did today or does every day.

Extended family: Create a family group on Facebook (or another network site) and invite everyone important and close to you to join it. Say, "I know I'm not that good about staying in touch right now. I hope in a few months life will be more sane. (Sleep will help!) In the meantime, thanks for your understanding and support. It means so much. I thought this might be a good way for me to touch base and hopefully to hear from you. Please do let me know what's going on in your life. I might be groggy and sleep-deprived, but I still love you and care! P.S. Here's the newest picture of the Princess/Prince."

Now you've set the stage for "quick touches" in the next few months—sweet! Then, each day, check your Facebook account and post something about your day and a photo, if you have one. See if your family members posted and respond to them too.

Undoubtedly, if you're close with your mother, this won't be everything she needs, so decide if you should have a quick daily call, or if you'll need to commit to a weekly hour-long call when your husband is around. Or if she lives in town, invite her over to hang out. You'll take off some pressure, however, if you do something like Facebook!

> *Friends:* What you just did for family (Facebook and so on) now do with your closest girlfriends. In the combined ten minutes you have for friends/family you can "touch" all of them! (Set a timer—those sites can absorb hours if you let them!)

Once a week, when you have backup support from Hubby, allot twenty minutes to call one of your closest friends and catch up. Start the conversation with, "Hey, I had twenty minutes and just wanted to hear your voice. How are things going for you?" (That way, your four closest pals are at least hearing from you once a month.)

> *Community/World:* Subscribe (use that orange RSS button) to a trusted blog, newsletter, or paper that addresses issues that matter to you. Scan headlines each day so you have some semblance of knowledge of what's going on! And find a mission organization that you care about; most will send you a daily or weekly eNewsletter (if you subscribe) and it will prompt you to pray for them—a way to take action as a globa-mama.

You see how it works? Even the stressed-out mom can work in this much time and energy on her relationships, and it will keep her from getting *more* fried because her loved ones are all hurt and angry! I call it preventive care. Just like you take your baby to the doctor for regular check-ups, solely to make sure all is developing right, so must you take care of your "village" and you. As life eases up, and you start breathing and sleeping again, take thirty to sixty minutes a day to stay in touch. It's amazing what good you can do in sixty minutes, spending just ten minutes on each of those most important relationships!

And soon you might even be able to steal away for a lunch with a girlfriend or an afternoon of shopping with your mom or, wait, brace yourself, a *weekend away on retreat* with those nice girls from church you've wanted to get to know but haven't had the chance. It all comes around in time. In the meantime, be patient and gentle with yourself. Adapt to the season, but be aware of changes in the air, in your schedule, changes that signal the transition of one season into another—don't let a *season* become a *lifetime*.

Value Relationships

You were never meant to live life on Planet Mom alone and disconnected. You were meant to have relationships, filled with joy and depth and meaning—something you want to model for your children too, right? It's important, this relationship thing. Whether you're an introvert or extrovert, quiet or loud, everyone craves connection, to know we're not alone. We need support to muddle through the confusing times, help to get through the hard times, and companions to help celebrate the best times.

They're out there, my friend—your God, your husband or future husband, your family, your pal, your community. And they need you, just as much as you need them. In the midst of taking such good care of your precious child(ren), don't forget to watch this front too.

So as I finish this book, I'm visualizing each of you across America, perhaps beyond, and I'm so thankful that you've spent the time with me here. I already feel as though you're a new friend of mine, ready to sit down to share a cup of coffee and chat. Here's my prayer for each of you:

Creator God, I pray for the woman holding this book in her hands. I ask that you cover her with your hands and help her take a long, deep breath. I pray that she will not see relationships as "just one more thing" to take care of, but she will see how each will ultimately take care of her and add to her life in fine, sweet ways. Show her, Papa God, what she needs to do on all those relationship fronts. And help her find the time and energy to do it. We love you and thank you for everything fine in our lives. Amen.

Notes

1. Stefanie Wilder-Taylor, *Sippy Cups Are Not for Chardonnay* (New York: Simon and Schuster, 2006), 2.

2. Lisa Whelchel, *Taking Care of the Me in Mommy* (Nashville: Thomas Nelson, 2006), xvi–xvii.

3. Elisa Morgan and Carol Kuykendall, *Children Change a Marriage* (Grand Rapids: Zondervan, 1999), 26–27.

4. H. Norman Wright and Sheryl Wright Macauley, *Making Peace with Your Mom* (Grand Rapids: Bethany, 2007), 17, italics mine.

5. Henry Cloud and John Townsend, *The Mom Factor* (Grand Rapids: Zondervan, 1996), 18.

6. John Cloud, "The Science of Experience," *Time*, March 10, 2008, 33.

7. Dee Brestin, *The Friendships of Women* (Colorado Springs: David C. Cook, 2008), 176, parenthetical addition mine.

8. Ibid., 183.

9. John Eldredge, *Walking with God* (Nashville: Thomas Nelson, 2008), ix.

Dear Reader,

In case you're wondering, I'm an author of mostly fiction and children's books, with a smattering of gift books and nonfiction in the mix, that have sold many more copies than I ever could have believed. I'm amazed at the doors that God has opened, including the opportunity to write this book. I promise that if you open your life to God—really open it—he'll take you on many more adventures than you would have guessed you could take. But life is not always an out-and-out adventure. Day to day I live a pretty normal, middle-class life in suburban Colorado Springs with my husband, Tim, a sculptor and Christian media arts professional, and our three children, Olivia (who is in middle school—high school by the time this book comes out!), Emma (elementary school), and Jack (preschool).

If you're not sick of me yet, and even possibly want to know more, you can take a look at my website at www. LisaTawnBergren.com and sign up for my monthly eNewsletter (prizes involved—trust me, it's worth it just for the potential goodies). Or join my online community at Facebook (just type in "Lisa Bergren" in the search box and you'll spot me). Given your momdom, you might also be particularly interested in my blog, www.BusyMomsDevo. com, where I post a new devotional or thought about once a week. It doesn't take a lot of time to read and it might be a way to make you think about God in a new way in the midst of your busy life. I'd love to stay connected with you in some way.

In any case, even if we never fall in step along the same road again, you have honored me by spending some of your precious time reading this book. Know I wish you every blessing along the mama journey and that I am really and truly praying for *you*. I've been at this long enough to understand that God takes my feeble words and sometimes makes them something unique that "speaks" to readers, but when that happens, that's him, not me.

And in that same way, he takes my prayers for my unseen "readers" and *sees* you, right where you are—with all your triumphs and failures, desires and disappointments—and touches you. He is the bridge between us. Isn't that the coolest? *That*, my friend, my sister, is *community* and *relationship* on a much broader scale. I love that. May you feel my hug through him *right now*!

Every good thing,

Lisa

Better together...

MOPS is here to come alongside you during this season of early mothering to give you the support and resources you need to be a great mom.

Get connected today!

Mothers of Preschoolers

2370 S. Trenton Way, Denver CO 80231
888.910.MOPS • www.MOPS.org/bettermoms

Mothering isn't just about the kids— it's a learning adventure for mom too!

the mommy diaries

finding yourself in the daily adventure

edited by tally flint

foreword by naomi cramer overton

president of MOPS International

Catch a fresh glimpse of who you are and how you can grow in the midst of being Mom.

Revell

a division of Baker Publishing Group
www.RevellBooks.com

Available wherever books are sold

Home business success is a reality!

Find out how to balance time between work and family, set realistic goals, and handle the challenges of being both "Mommy" and "The Boss" while running a profitable home-based business.

Perfect Gifts for a New Mom!

New moms run into a host of new challenges once baby arrives. The New Mom's Guides go straight to the heart of these matters, offering moms guidance and encouragement in this new season of life.